TH

— ⁊⁊ —

INCONVENIENT

— ⁊⁊ —

TRUTH

— ⁊⁊ —

OF

— ⁊⁊ —

CHURCH HURT

Sussy,
Thank you for your
support! I pray this
Book brings enlightenment
and deepened Compassion!

CONTESSA BROWN

ISBN 978-1-0980-8394-6 (paperback)
ISBN 978-1-0980-8395-3 (digital)

Christian Faith Publishing, Inc.
832 Park Avenue
Meadville, PA 16335
www.christianfaithpublishing.com

Pearls cover photo credit: Jamal & Lashana Photography
Author's photo credit: Ronny Cabrera

Printed in the United States of America

DEDICATION

I dedicate the book to...

My mom, Janne't Brown, who is the heartbeat of every dream and vision I birth. You have given me life and spoken life in me. When life thought it was throwing me lemons, you taught me how to find the tree to make it my shade.

To my love Ronny Cabrera, who is my prayer and life partner, my motivator, my balance and blessing.

To my friends and family who have witnessed this walk and encouraged me to remain authentic and true.

To the wounded. May this book plant an incorruptible seed of healing.

CONTENTS

FOREWORD

Personally, seeing through my own lens, the unflinching examination of the church's brokenness—from insensitive bureaucracy to the deep scars left permanently upon many.

Knowing the story behind *The Inconvenient Truth*, I promise you, it's the TRUTH, as well as it offers moving stories, helpful perspectives, and healthy ways forward, which provides honest insight for a psychologically wise and spiritually profound path forward for Christians who have experienced the deep pain being abused, traumatized, or wounded by other Christians in the church, especially those in leadership. Contessa writes out of her own and others' personal experiences of finding surprising and powerful grace and healing in the darkest of places. It took courage for Contessa to write with such honesty and transparency, including the testimonies of real members of the wounded Body of Christ and the pain they have experienced. Her courage will give you courage, the courage to confront the facts of sin and weakness within the church.

Fearless in her assessment, Contessa is equally confident that in God, Jesus Christ, and the Holy Spirit, you can move toward healing and wholeness and allow you to discover Him once again within the embrace of a new home church, despite the failings of previous church leaders and members.

The Inconvenient Truth is a must-read for Christians as it shows us how to live up to our identity as a church that goes out proactively to bring Christ's healing to those who are wounded. God bless!

Janne't Brown
Co-Founding Partner and Chief Operating
Officer of Café S.O.U.L.™
June 2020

PRELUDE
CHURCH

We have a problem. It's a big one. Even worse, it's a silent killer; and it seems no one is supposed to talk about it. Unfortunately, the silent killer is often woven into the fabric of this problem, which is one of the primary reasons why so few will risk even entering the conversation. But instead of talking about "it", we talk around "it", and thus the epidemic grows. There are many "Church Caucuses" that play a huge role in the attitude, politics, and manipulation among the church leadership and congregation. I hope to shed some light on the darkness of an issue affecting literally millions of people every year. It's important to talk about the uncomfortable, the risky, the shameful, and then hope, help, and healing are available for ones that attempt to seek it.

The Silent Killer of One's Spirit within a Church

The unforgettable disrespect by a church one attended is very painful. It doesn't mean that the words and events that burned and hurt one's heart are not very ugly and public. In fact, this is why I call it the silent killer, because of what it does deep in the fabric of the mind, heart, and soul of the wounded. If not dealt with, it will destroy future happiness, joy, and well-being. The collateral damage always negatively affects the ministry and outreach of the church, too, and some churches never recover. Recognize that the behavior which brought such devastation in one's heart is not much different than the hurt any of us can encounter in the workplace, marketplace, or home. The difference is that one doesn't expect God's people to behave like those without Christ in one's life. The church is one place almost everyone agrees should be safe, accepting, forgiving, and free from conflict, jealousy, and pain. I must say, in most churches, at least some elements of strife, conflict, and hatred creep in and shatter that dream.

I'm sure many realize it's in more churches than others. The spiritual health of people in a church and the strength of leadership determine how prevalent and to what extent that divisive behavior can gain control. Out of control, it has the effect of a termite infiltration that slowly decays the foundation of the spiritual life of a congregation.

It's important to turn one's focus away from the people involved and the church itself and identify the root cause of one's pain, turmoil, and disillusionment. If you are like most, the possibilities can be anger, disappointment, rejection, hurt feelings, jealousy, threatened, fear, rebellion, pride, feeling foolish, ashamed, embarrassed, blamed, and loss. One must find out the core of one's hurt—not what someone said or did to you, but what is really causing one's pain.

Then, read the Bible and look up scriptures to discover what God says about what is really hurting you. For example, one may think that oneself is angry, when in reality, you feel rejected. What does God say about rejection? "Never will I leave you; never will I forsake you" (Hebrews 13:5).

When one truly finds the root of one's pain, God has a balm of wisdom, compassion, and love to generously apply to heal your wound(s). When one calls on God for this, one's focus quickly becomes riveted on Him rather than on someone else or dwelling on and rehearsing the event over and over that caused one harm. Being honest with one's self, one may be harmed, injured, or offended. One certainly feels it. Which are by-products of deeper, more important realities that have derailed one's passion for God, His church, and His purpose for one's life. This has soured one's taste, and if unattended, it will lead to a root of bitterness that will negatively affect every fiber of your soul and will rob you of any possibility of finding fulfillment in Christ. Don't allow this to happen in one's life.

One should read the Book of Wisdom from the Bible which says, one must "guard one's heart above all else, for it determines the course of one's life" (Proverbs 4:23). One guards one's heart by choosing the thoughts, feelings, attitudes, and actions we hold. Guard one's heart in this situation by refusing to rehearse what happened over and over, dwelling on the people who hurt you. It will take the power of the Holy Spirit working in and through one's self (Ephesians 3:16).

Never ever blame God for how his children behave. Don't abandon going to church either. There are many more dedicated, grace-filled, loving, and forgiving people in most churches than you think. Seek them out, spend time with them, learn about their ministry, mission, and credentials. You wouldn't go to a doctor or a bank you do not know anything about. Be careful who spiritually deposits into you and spiritually heals you. If one can't find them, find another church. The church is God's idea, and He protects it faithfully even though He is pained often by its behavior. One must always stay prayed over and remain prayed up.

Please understand many have had and still have a wound of this magnitude, and if unattended, it will continually penetrate deeply into one's soul and destroy any chance of living and finding the purpose of one's life! Many can have faith and hope when seeking healing through having a spiritual one-on-one relationship with God. I close my thought with one of my favorite Scriptures when one needs comfort: "Come to me, all you who are weary and burden, and I will give you rest. Take my yoke upon you and learn from Me, for I am gentle and humble in heart, and you will find rest for your souls. For my yoke is easy and my burden is light" (Jesus Christ, Matthew 11:28–30).

Janne't.
December 17, 2014

INTRO

I invite you to come with me through my journey along with twelve other persons' journey in this walk of life called Christianity. Now what I am about to unfold on the next few pages is not out of anger and spite. This is not a tirade or bratty impulse disguised as literature. This is truth that needs light to be shed upon. Unfortunately, it is taboo to discuss these topics in church or about church. But it is time to be REAL! There are people hurting from past pains caused by church folk. They are ready for realness and not pretentiousness. It is time to shed light on what is inconvenient for some, to dig deep and reflect on or look in the mirror and reevaluate. It is time to talk about this inconvenient yet real and raw truth. Yes, there will be some tea spillage in this book but not as gossip. These true life experiences are near and dear to each person's heart and soul.

What fueled the start of this book: my own painful experience with a particular church. In fact, this book is nearly ten years in the making. I had to go through an evolvement that needed my involvement in healing. This healing took place through redefining my own relationship with God, going through life's hardships to curate humility, experience healing through mental wellness techniques introduced through grad school, and finding a church I can call home. Now, that is my tailored journey. Everyone's journey to healing will be as unique as the fingertips that touch this book's pages.

Of course, while putting together this project and scribing my thoughts, there was push back. I had one indicate that what I am doing is no better than the devout Christian person bashing and hurting. However, my thought is this, we need to stop making things seem prettier than it really is. When in fact, these sugar-coated events that constantly occur without getting addressed continue to make the pain be prolonged and festered. My response is not that this is an eye for an eye, nor an issue with a plank in my eye while focusing on someone else's speck in theirs. This is iron sharpening iron so we can know where we went wrong so we can make it right.

The intention of this book is to peek into the lives of those who have been hurt, to evaluate our past and current pains, our past and current actions, and to see in what ways can we grow more compassionate, caring, understanding, and thoughtful. There are parts in the book where you will be able to pause and reflect. I truly want you, as readers, to be engaged. I want this book to be thought-provoking as well as a life changer. This book will challenge those with rigid religious beliefs, but it is for the betterment and wellness of everyone.

How this book will be set-up is, first, into my own personal journey, and then to follow the case studies in which I will reference as integrated summaries of people who participated in an interview. Like the twelve disciples, there are a total of twelve participants. Like HIPAA, to protect names and business entities, different names will be used. Intertwined in these journeys will be a series of questions that will give you an opportunity to pause and reflect as well as possibly resonate with the person's case study.

So find a nice relaxed place to curl up and read this book with your favorite beverage of choice—wine, coffee, or maybe even tea. Also, have a pen ready to pour your thoughts through ink into the pages.

NOTE: In the event that some of these stories are triggering, please honor yourself and take a pause. Put the book down and refer to the breathing techniques in the **Closure-or-Non-Closure?** section of the book. There will also be a page of resources you can refer to for your emotional and mental wellness. I also encourage you to have a separate personal journal to write out any emotions, memories, affirmations, confirmations, you name it. I had a writing teacher who said whenever you hear an interesting word or phrase write it down. I not only invite you to write down what piques your interests, but also what piques your emotional and physical responses.

Countess' Journey

Chuuuuuuuch: The Invitation

"If you are going to sleep over under this roof, you are going to church in the morning," said Ms. Harmony, my friend's mom. Church? I had not been to church since my grandma's funeral in May 1999. I went the next day to service, and my perception of church was changed entirely. See, I was not raised in the church, but my mom always had strong faith and the Bible by her bedside. I remember when I was like five or six years old, I used to attend Spanish services with my cousins. I didn't understand a lick of Spanish, but I felt the presence of God. I swear I used to randomly smell dry roses, and it made me feel like God was near. When I was a teenager, I knew about the Bible, but I didn't understand what having a relationship with Him was like. I only went to church with my friends because it was playtime. It was time that we could go get Frooties candy by Schrimshaw's and giggle in the back of church, until we got that motherly eye from the sisters in front. I will be very honest, church was boring to me as a child. So disengaging and playing childish games was more fun, obviously.

It was not until that day Ms. Harmony invited me to church that I truly gained an understanding of who God was. The Bible started to make sense to me and was no longer a book that danced in the dust of the corner shelf.

୨୦୯ଓ

When I was a child, I spoke as a child, I understood as a child, I thought as a child; but when I became a man, I put away childish things.

1 Corinthians 13:11 NKJV

୨୦୯ଓ

This invitation was granted to me exactly seven years after my grandma passed that I reconnected with faith and God. The church I was attending was in Newport, Rhode Island. But it was starting to become harder and harder to go to on Sundays. I had to get up at 6:00 AM to take two buses just to be there on time for service. So naturally, I needed to find a church that was more close to my newfound home, Providence, Rhode Island, the creative city. I was referred to a local church in 2007. Although I was still tangoing with the nightclubs and men, I started to become more and more intrigued and enlightened by this newfound faith. I was transformed and also conformed. Conforming to what I thought Christianity should look and sound like. I started attending church like it was work. Sunday to Saturday I was there for every ministry fathomable. From worship team rehearsal, to youth ministry, Bible study, women's ministry, Friday night prayer, you name it! No pun intended. Like any relationship, the more you spend time with people, the more you build trust and bond. This church was what I considered to be like a family, so I thought. My thought patterns started to change and mirror the mindset of that particular church. Adopting certain beliefs and teachings where some were Bible-based and some were simply rigid religion and ideologies. I began to put myself on a pedestal as well as put the leaders in that church on an even higher pedestal. I, in turn, hurt people with my own mouth; evil and wicked tongue. I judged, I ridiculed, and I isolated persons in my life. A few years later, I had a friend tell me that the reason why they had not spoken to me in years was because of my words; it was the way I said it. I said it with great disdain and disgust, rather than allowing it to be a teachable and reachable moment. He understood where my intention was rooted, but he expressed that he would have accepted my point of view had I delivered it differently, with kindness and respect.

|| PRESSPAUSE

&)C&

I would like to take the time to openly apologize to those whom I have offended in the past with my actions and words. I do not expect this to wipe away your permanent tears and hurt. I also do not expect you to accept my apology. I just want you to know my sincerity in my apology. It took for God to humble me by getting hurt by church leadership to truly tear the plank out of my eye so that I can see and be more compassionate, more relatable, more REAL.

NOT EVERYONE READS THE BIBLE. PEOPLE KNOW OF THE BIBLE EITHER AS A BOOK, THE GOOD BOOK, BASIC INSTRUCTIONS BEFORE LEAVING EARTH. SOME ARE NOT INTERESTED IN READING THE BOOK. PEOPLE WILL READ YOU, YOUR AURA, YOUR ENERGY, YOUR ATTITUDE, AND THE WORDS THAT COME OUT OF YOUR MOUTH. YOU MAY BE THE ONLY BIBLE THEY WILL EVER READ. IT IS IMPERATIVE THAT WE TREAT PEOPLE WITH RESPECT AND SPEAK WITH WORDS OF KINDNESS AND WITH INTENT RATHER THAN HATRED AND ILL WILL.

&)C&

TRUTH MOMENT: There was a moment in my Bible-thumping days where I offended friends close to me. One of my friends who is gay had revealed to me why he had stopped talking to me for so many years. It was a time when he invited me to a gay bar and the answer I gave to him at that time was hurtful. He explained that he understood what my beliefs were at that time, but it was the way I replied to him. I replied in a manner that was with utter disgust in my facial expressions and words. This hurt him for a very long time. I was confronted with my own truth. I accepted it, and I apologized. **#Humbled.**

I went to a women's breakfast in April 2011. The topic was about birthing your dream and that we need a team to help us birth the team, from the nurse, to the doctor, to the nutritionist, etc. Ironically, earlier that morning, I prayed to God that I needed more people on my team for Café S.O.U.L. There was a prophetic word given to me that there was going to be a young gay man that is going to support Café S.O.U.L. with such passion. She said when he comes to me, I must accept him with open arms and love. I accepted the prophetic word because I was much more open-minded and accepting at that point. I wasn't sure who this young man was, and for years after, I had wondered who this young man is, as he has not shown up in my life yet. He did not appear to me yet because my heart needed to be molded and mind needed to be renewed. It needed to be ridded of the rigid heartless dogma I learned from previous teachings. I needed to adhere to the teachings of Christ and love unconditionally not only my neighbors, but especially, my loved ones. It didn't appear to me that the young man she was talking about was my very best friend. My best friend whose mom encouraged me to go back to church and my best friend who put a fire under my butt to birth Café S.O.U.L. He was the doula of my dreams and the godfather of my vision. It was years later where he felt safe enough and comfortable enough to reveal to me his sexual identity. In order for me to truly embrace him, I needed to endure pain through church hurt, failed relationships, and joblessness. **#Humbled**.

℘CR

"I do not judge people by the scriptures of their faith or the scars from their past, I embrace them by the content of their hearts"

—Dodinsky

℘CR

REFLECT

In what ways have you been hurt by a person of faith? As a person of faith, have you hurt someone knowingly? Take time to write your thoughts.

_____

_____

_____

_____

_____

_____

_____

_____

_____

_____

_____

_____

_____

_____

_____

_____

_____

_____

_____

_____

_____

_____

_____

_____

_____

_____

_____

➢ PRESSPLAY

Chuuuuuuuuuch Ministry

As I got more comfortable with the church, I started a ministry in 2009 called Café S.O.U.L. It originally started off as a singles ministry. But because I did not want to exclude married couples, I expanded it to young adults and adults ages seventeen and up. The vision was always to bring people together through art, music, and food in a clean environment, no alcohol. I also wanted something more fun to do as a single young adult Christian. Let's be real, bowling and roller-skating can be a bit juvenile. I wanted to have classy grown-folk fun. Especially because at that time, when I was freshly a reborn Christian, I thought I needed to drop all forms of fun cold turkey. Now of course, a few years later, I decided I knew what was best for me and my walk in Christ. I occasionally go out to dance and have a drink. I have even begun to like bowling again. My vice was never clubs and alcohol, and personally I don't like to twerk in public (inside joke).

ഇൻ

Let no one look down on [you because of] your youth but be an example and set a pattern for the believers in speech, in conduct, in love, in faith, and in [moral] purity.

1 TIMOTHY 4:12

AMP

ഇൻ

When I first began the ministry Café S.O.U.L. everything was running so lovely and so smooth. Honeymoon phase. Vision was set and everyone who was in leadership was on board. But I should have known that the fabric of this vision was going to get nicked and picked at along the way where on the very first night, my close and dear Muslim friend who rode his bike through three cities to get to the church to perform was asked by the pastor to just sit in the crowd and not participate. It was then explained to me that the "spirit" of the person is not right and they cannot be on the microphone and the audience cannot be under their influence. Me, being the somewhat open-minded and hopeful person, responded back indicating I understand we are Spirit beings, but with a God that is omnipresent, God can influence whomever is on the microphone and speak directly to their spirit. We never know what God can do between the speaker and that microphone. There were times where my venues were purposely interrupted. For example, I had a friend who was reciting his poem that beautifully painted how the Lord rescued him from committing suicide. Right in the midst of his poetic testimony, leaders decided they wanted to build a kitchen island in the back room, banging and clanging the parts together so loud that it drowned out his lyrics. Because he was flamboyant and effeminate, as they kept stating over and over in a leadership board meeting, he should not have been speaking on the microphone. Little did they know that effeminate and passionate man's father is a pastor who loves him dearly. I just about lost it that night because prior to the venue commencing, the pastor tells me that the artist whom I had booked for a month is not able to have her art exhibited in the church. The art was to open minds about the apocrypha, the missing books of the Bible. I was told this right when my guest was almost done setting up her exhibition, and I had to tell her she had to break the setup down. Fast forward to later that evening, once we left, the elders and pastors that oversaw the venue were "spiritually" cleansing out the sanctuary as if we just defiled it. They did not want me to have persons on the mic that spoke, looked, acted, smelled differently than they do. I once had a lady who dressed masculine come to an open mic. Her poetry was so amazing and God-centered but because her appearance was not "God-centered" according to the leadership, they asked me not to have her come to speak again. "These people" who are deemed different are the very people outside the four walls of church that we are trying to reach out to and love. Let God do the cleansing and what He sees fit for their life and journey. Who are we to judge? Once again, "these people" were children of God who had faith in God and spoke truth and enlightenment. I was so hurt because of the way they pushed away precious souls. Café S.O.U.L. is founded on Christian beliefs but is NOT a church. Café S.O.U.L. serves as an alternative outlet in the social scene and is open to all people of all walks of life. That church started to pull the strings of the woven vision God gave me. They said I was too young to hear from God; a ripe age of twenty-five. Did they not recall King David that they preached about on Sunday morning? How about Hezekiah? He was twenty-five years old when he assumed the role of a king. I feel like I could relate to him. I will touch more upon that later.

Each time I had to meet with the leaders to gain their unsolicited judgmental advice and feedback of the ministry, I always felt like I was in the lion's den being slayed with irrelevant Bible verses and manmade ideologies laced with a few positive highlights of the venue. Never mind the fact that the attendees' poetry was uplifting and positive because people in the crowd would be too focused on the way the person was dressed like a man but voice was of a woman or vice versa. I was so fed up with their judgmental ways, but I bit my tongue and remained "humble."

The Turning Point

MAY 22, 2010, a date that will indelibly remain engraved in the crevices of my memories and thoughts. This was to be a day to celebrate the second published book of one of my brotha from anotha motha (New England accent for ya). A night that he can truly find his voice. Instead, this was an evening where I found my voice again. As a human being, we all have this feeling that is housed within us. A moral compass and a true gut feeling that senses the good and the bad. A pastor had invited in an intoxicated relative to the venue. One thing that is not permitted at Café S.O.U.L. is intoxicated persons because havoc will follow. I figured since this is her relative, then he can be trusted. He was hovering over the music equipment, and I knew something was not right. He attempted to leave, and I had a feeling that my iPod was missing. I went to the sound table and, lo and behold, the iPod that was used to provide music for Café S.O.U.L.'s venue was no longer there! So I approached this man and kindly asked him for my iPod. I tried to remain humble, and he humbly lied to my face. So something within me had enough! From the previous weeks of my venues being sabotaged, I had enough! So a boldness emerged within me, and I locked the front door and exclaimed no one is leaving until the iPod is returned! I literally went head to head with this man and was finally standing up for myself. Because previously, I was brainwashed to think being humbled is equated to being a doormat and you just had to take what people did to you. I had it! I was no longer going to accept what people within the church were doing to me! So I decided that day was the day my voice will be found again. I demanded what was mine to be returned. I demanded respect because Countess was no longer taking anyone's mess. This ex-diva became a diva again but with a purpose. Being an heir of God does not mean that we have to allow the enemy to come into our palace and take whatever he pleases.

This mini victory was not seen like that by the church members. Rather, they blamed me for putting the church at a dangerous stake; never mind why an intoxicated person was invited into the venue in the first place by one of the leaders! We shunned and turned away homosexuals and Muslims who do no harm and not allow them to participate in venues,

ಸಿಞ

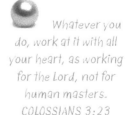

Whatever you do, work at it with all your heart, as working for the Lord, not for human masters.
COLOSSIANS 3:23

ಸಿಞ

but we can allow a person intoxicated with liquid spirits to come into a venue and stir ruckus? Something is twisted, and thank God I had my true friends and family at the venue who have already witnessed the mess I had "humbly" put up with, who understood where I was coming from and celebrated with me the victory of finding my TRUE self in God. No longer was I going to blindly follow. No! I will ask questions, and I will make sure to come into an understanding of who God is and what His word means truly for myself. This was the revolutionary turn for Countess. But to the church, this was rebelliousness. So they cancelled my venue for a month in fear that the intoxicated person that their pastor allowed into the premises may retaliate back. I was so used to my previous venues being sabotaged before that I went through with it. That month I decided to start planning for the one year anniversary. What progressed the months later produced the head of the monster to show its true ugly character.

Digression. The night prior is when I was introduced to a new church body that encompassed everything I prayed for in a church. I attended their youth night that I was invited to come to and share my poetry. My eyes were opened to a new kind of freedom in Christ. Whenever I heard the pastor of the church playing Musiq Soulchild on his iPod, I was like YES! (Yaaaaaaaaaaas was not in then, LOL.) This is the church body that is revolutionary in their approach, and it aligned with Café S.O.U.L.'s very vision. I saw myself being a part of this church body, but I was already in a committed relationship to a church, that although was emotionally and mentally hurting me, I could not step out. You can only step out when you know enough is enough.

AUGUST 2010

It almost came time for Café S.O.U.L.'s one year anniversary! [Insert excitement, right?] I explained to the head leader of the church that I would not be able to attend the church's annual summer picnic, a picnic I attended all three summers previously. That leader started to yell at me and waving his ego in the air with statements such as, "Are you the bishop? No, I am the bishop, and I say what goes on around here!" My apologies that I am not able to fellowship one day out of the seven days of the week I am always here. My apologies I serve a God of decency and order and He created me so wonderfully that I have to be organized and set up to make sure the venue is presented with excellence (Colossians 3:23).

Well, the next step of course is that he cancelled the one-year anniversary that I had spent two months preparing for, from booking artists to getting sponsors for the event, etc. This appeared to spur from my cancellation from going to a church picnic, which I went to every single summer for three years. Except, this year I needed to cancel so I could prepare the night before for Café S.O.U.L.'s one-year anniversary. This seemed to conjure up deep-rooted feelings in the head pastor. He lashed at me screaming, "You are not the church leader, I AM! I could care less about what your mother has to say, she isn't a part of this church!" In essence, that I was not the one running the show and his power was the almighty. Additionally, the same day he was scorning me for to soothe his ego, I had a venue set for that very night. A venue planned for the very evening he decided to cancel the one-year anniversary celebration. I had to bite my tongue so hard until I felt the blood on the tip of it. Let me tell you, that event ending up being my very last event at that church. That place was packed like an Easter Sunday service. So many gifted artists blessing the mic and painting the crowd and atmosphere with their melodic words and songs. The expression of the pastors was priceless, as they were in awe of the amazing ministry that they attempted to abort was prosperous.

|| PRESSPAUSE

Now I know people may think that this is a rant or that I left because I did not get my way. Firstly and most importantly, I did seek the Lord to see if I should stay or go. I was released by my Father and sought spiritual covering at another church organization immediately. What I have experienced at this particular church did not deter me from seeking spiritual cover from another church home. Rather, it challenged my point of view. Rather than putting pastors upon pedestals, I was able to see their human and inhumane side.

Secondly, I have to answer to my Lord, and when He asks why did I not proceed with the vision that He gave me as He instructed me to do, I can't say, "But pastor so-and-so said" or "Elder so-and-so said" or "Bishop so-and-so said." NO! He will state, "But what did I tell you?" I could not keep allowing them to keep pulling the strings until the vision was unwoven and shredded to pieces. There are hurt souls out there waiting to be fed. Café S.O.U.L. is that creative way to deliver that message to them as well as allow their voices to be heard. The persons who they insulted were hurt and did not come back to Café S.O.U.L. for a while. In the process, I was also hurt by the way I was treated, especially my baby, my child Café S.O.U.L. Anyone who knows me knows that I do not have human children, but Café S.O.U.L. she was conceived and birthed by the vision God planted in my womb.

➢ PRESSPLAY

When I was given permission by my Father to leave, I requested to have an exit interview with the pastors. I was denied the exit interview because I already made my mind and decision. The purpose of an exit interview is so that the person who is opting to leave the congregation to communicate their reason for leaving the church and the leadership's responsibility is to see how they can mend the relationship as well as gauge at what they are doing well and what opportunities of improvement they have within the ministry and congregation.

When I went to go and collect my items from the church that same week, it was such a dreary feeling. I walked up to the pastor's office for one last time. There was no greeting, not even a factitious greeting. The head pastor, with a straight, stern, and cold face, parted his lips to only ask if my items tucked in the corner were mine, if I purchased all those items, and to return the key. That's the end of that relationship. I was heartbroken. Literally, I had to go to Miriam hospital due to chest pains and heart palpitations.

Ironically, the pastors told the congregation that they had to ask me to leave the church because I was rebellious and that I was of a wicked spirit. Even told members of that congregation to no longer talk to me or attend any of my events. Firstly, how does a church of God ask someone to leave His house? Excommunication? Secondly, if anyone knew me, I was so by-the-book, by-the-Bible, Bible-thumping Christian at THAT time, had they seen my journey a few years later, yes, they could have the liberty of calling me rebellious. In fact, like Hezekiah, I started off on good footing and did as God led me to do at a young age. But then, I started to become arrogant. Now Hezekiah was prideful and arrogant toward the Lord toward the end of his reign. He thought what he was doing was honoring God during his reign as king. I was not arrogant to the leaders. This arrogance had seeped after I left that particular congregation. While searching for new meaning, redefining my relationship with God, and healing, I started to become arrogant to the signs and warnings God was speaking to me when it came to relationships with men. I started to ignore the red flags and became arrogant when I was being recognized and pursued by men, in the midst of my pain from church hurt and disappointment. What happened later down the line, I will further expound in my next book on dating and courtship. I digress. NO, I was considered rebellious because I finally decided NOT to be a doormat and to speak my mind, question teachings I either needed clarity on or did not sit well with my soul. I was rebellious because I wanted to extend services to those who were Muslim, gay, or lesbian, those who wanted to teach new things. Lastly, I was rebellious because all the while, when I was seeking to use their 501c3 so I can obtain funding to get Café S.O.U.L. a 501c3, it was revealed that that church at that time was not even using their own 501c3, but a 501c3 from another church outside the state of Rhode Island. So because I had that cup of tea, they started to treat me differently.

||PRESSPAUSE

BACK SLIDDEN

Definition: To lapse into bad habits or vices from a state of virtue, religious faith, etc. [1]

When I left the church, although I found another church to get spiritual covering, I also was trying to find my own path. It was a new type of freedom to redefine who Contessa was. No more constraints of the churches dos and don'ts and thous. I was searching for my true authentic self and identity. While navigating

---

[1] Backslide definition from https://www.thefreedictionary.com/backslidden

this newfound freedom, I entered into relationships that plucked, pruned, and groomed me. I started to wear more scantily clothing, clubbing more, and broke my three-and-a-half-year celibacy. Now, don't get me wrong, I still like to show a little cleavage here and there and rip the rug from time to time on the dance floor. But at that time, it is with a different intention. Then I went to clubs to get attention from men. I dressed the way I dressed to get attention from men. But I had to go through a whirlwind of relationships to be content with being me by myself and rebuild my relationship with Christ.

TRUTH MOMENT: I wanted to leave that confession with you. As we are not perfect, nor do we strive for perfection. We strive for patience. We are human beings striving to teach the world the love of Jesus.

Overall, we must do the work within ourselves in order to produce the changes we desire to see. We have to do the self-evaluation and reflection. Take responsibility for only what we can take responsibility for and work through or find ways to cope with the pain and hurt.

My entire identity was consumed by what they taught me I SHOULD or OUGHT to be. I was not my true authentic self.

➤ PRESSPLAY

August 13, 2011

A year later, the Lord had given me insight on a way I can gain closure. I prayed for a date. I went to a service, and the sermon was about cleaning the closet and dealing with stored away issues, stemming from the scripture Romans 8:13, "For if you live according to the flesh, you will die; but if by the Spirit you put to death the misdeeds of the body, you will live." In essence, we cannot approach a situation through our carnal nature. We must approach any situation and issue through the Spirit. I then decided the date to meet should be August 13, 2011. I had e-mailed them to let them know I forgave them, and they never responded. I left it at that.

Now, you may ask if I forgave them, then why I am writing this book? Once again, this is to shed light on where as Christians we can do better. Forgiveness does not mean to completely forget. The purpose of this book is to be used as a guide of reflection. Reflect on our lives on how are we treating others and how are we being treated. I soon learned that this too is TRAUMA. Trauma comes in many different forms and can unconsciously shape our tomorrows. It is time to start reclaiming our voice and speaking about our experiences. Besides, it is the law of reciprocity. If you look in many of the different books of guidance and proverbs, the one precept that is common is do unto others as you would like to be done to you.

|| PRESSPAUSE

The previous church congregation did a number on me. As previously mentioned, I did find spiritual covering under another church body. I had let them know about the pain I endured with the previous church encounter. I let them know I was going to take my time getting involved into ministries and that Café S.O.U.L. is my baby. They were very understanding and supportive. My time at the church for the most part was great. I joined a few ministries, one in particular which was responsible for chiming in with members who are sick or who we have not seen in a while. Paradoxically, when I was in a near fatal car accident or became jobless, I did not receive any wellness visits or phone calls. I lived right up the street. I just graduated with my master's degree and not much of a word except a Facebook post. I am a part of Generation X, but my soul is old-fashioned. I guess this is where expectations come in, which we will briefly discuss later.

Closure or Non-Closure?

TRUTH MOMENT: I must admit that one of my biggest pet peeves is when some of my brothers and sisters in Christ are SO spiritual that they cannot admit their faults and SIMPLY apologize. There is no need for all this highfalutin language with sprinkles of irrelevant scripture. Rather, what needs to come out is an apology.

So what happens if you are not able to get the closure you are seeking? A pastor from another congregation taught me that sometimes, like the flower petals she had me toss in the sky, you must let the expectation of closure go because some will never grant it to you. How you can grant yourself closure is through forgiveness. Now, as cliché as it may sound, forgiveness is not for them, but it is for you; there is a huge kernel of truth in that. It is you that still has to deal with the pain and harbor feelings of anger and sadness. This can impact your overall health physically, mentally, emotionally, and spiritually. I want to invite you to think about a few things and write it down.

REFLECT

What would closure look like for you? What if you are not able to obtain closure, how does that make you feel?

_____
_____
_____
_____
_____
_____
_____
_____
_____
_____
_____

What does forgiveness mean to you? What would that look like?

_____
_____
_____
_____
_____
_____
_____
_____
_____
_____
_____
_____
_____
_____

In this section, I invite you to do a mindfulness exercise with some breathing techniques. When completing this exercise, please be sure to be alone without any distractions for about thirty minutes. Make yourself comfortable. Feel free to refer to the emotional word bank at the back of the book to assist with identifying your feelings. If these feelings start to become overwhelming, feel free to stop at any time.

Breathing Technique Steps[2]

1. Breathe in through your nose. Let your belly fill with air.
2. Breathe out through your nose.
3. Place one hand on your belly. Place the other hand on your chest.
4. As you breathe in, feel your belly rise. As you breathe out, feel your belly lower. The hand on your belly should move more than the one that's on your chest.
5. Take three more full, deep breaths. Breathe fully into your belly as it rises and falls with your breath.

Mindfulness Exercise

- Take a moment to think about someone whom you cannot seem to find an ounce of forgiveness.
- Take a deep breath and pay attention to what feelings or emotions arise.
- Take notice of body sensations such as sweating, tension, heart palpitations, clenched fists.

---

[2] Breathing Techniques from https://www.webmd.com/balance/stress-management/stress-relief-breathing-techniques#1

- Now write about it. What were your physical reactions? What emotions came up? (See emotional word bank at the back of the book.)

_____
_____
_____
_____
_____
_____
_____
_____
_____
_____
_____
_____
_____
_____
_____
_____
_____
_____
_____
_____
_____
_____
_____
_____
_____
_____
_____
_____
_____

PRAY

Some may be intimidated by the word pray because they believe they do not know how to pray. Some believe that prayers must be recited eloquent words. It can be that. But I invite and reinvite my readers to come to know that prayer is simply a conversation between you and the Lord. Just like a conversation you would have with your friend. Even if you cannot utter the words, He can sense it through your tears of joy and pain. Do not allow how others pray intimidate you, and do not allow others to criticize how you pray. Like all relationships, how you communicate with the person you are in the relationship is built upon how you both have come to understand and know one another. It is the same with God, you come to an understanding of who He is and communicate with Him in your true authentic ways. He created you and KNOWS you and certainly understands you.

Prayer of Forgiveness

Father God, please gaze into my heart and heal it from any pain I have ensured. Help me to forgive those who have hurt me knowingly and unknowingly, willingly and unwillingly. Father God, forgive me if I have knowingly and unknowingly, willingly and unwillingly hurt anyone and heal their heart so that they can forgive me too should they choose.

"Until the lion learns how to write, every story will glorify the hunter."
—African Proverb

Poetry Corner

As I Am
Contessa Brown
(November 20, 2010)

"Just take me as I am or have nothing at all. Just take as I am or have nothing at all."[3]
Who are you to judge?
When it's really over a matter of a grudge.
I apologize that this picture has a smudge,
When you assumed it would be perfect.
It's like you throw insults at me to
Protect what lies behind your doors
Because, see, lies come from behind your lips
and seep out your pores.
See, it took me a long time to like who I am.
Let me say it again!
It took me a long time to like who I am.
Who God already crafted and molded and destined me to be.
So,
"Just take me as I am or have nothing at all. Just take as I am or have nothing at all."
Better yet,
Say nothing at all if it's not to build me up and edify,
Just to justify your insecurities.

---

[3] Line from Mary J. Blige's song "Take Me as I Am" from *The Breakthrough* album.

Security! Please get this stalker who constantly gossips about me, like paparazzi.
Constantly watching every move that I make.
Not to ensure I am upright.
But to look for mistakes to point out.
Don't criticize me because I am FREE.
Free like a dove that flows above, showing unconditional love like JESUS.
I am living for He
And not for thee.
Just in case you missed that, I am living for Jehovah Elohim
And not for her or him.
Besides, I have to walk the path He has etched out for me,
And not the path He chose for you or you, but ME.
"Just take me as I am or have nothing at all. Just take as I am or have nothing at all."
You seem so appalled at what I speak.
But see, I found my voice, a voice previously taken without a choice.
I have strengthened the cords of this microphone
And have obtained confidence to speak up and speak OUT
Boldly, yet gentle
Respectable and backed up by the TRUTH.
Besides, you only came in at the end of the movie.
So I don't need your credits or for you to approve of me.
I just need you to
"Just take me as I am or have nothing at all. Just take as I am or have nothing at all."

Poetry is very cathartic and is a great vehicle to express emotions and thoughts. I invite you to start writing a piece for yourself below. You may choose to share this or not. The important thing here is that you are releasing those emotions and thoughts.

_____

_____

_____

_____

_____

_____

_____

_____

_____

_____

_____

_____

_____

_____

_____

_____

ഇ)ര

"Voir dire!" means to speak the truth in French.

ഇ)ര

➤ PRESSPLAY

Serendipitous as it may be, the very next year, that Muslim friend of mine and I got to perform poetry at a local university for a Christian-based concert. I cannot explain how excited it made me feel. It was like sweet revenge. As we were approaching the university, my heart kept racing like it was when I had first left the church. My soul was sensing some type of energy, and I didn't know what it was. When I got to the concert, the pastors were in attendance. Frozen in time like a Del's lemonade, I wasn't sure what I would do. It is almost like that moment in Tyler Perry's *Why Did I Get Married?* and Jill Scott's character, Sheila, sees the woman her ex-husband committed adultery with. She said to her she wondered what she would do if she had the chance to see her again. But she remained poised, calm, and unbothered. She was courteous and cordial. Well, that was my same exact response. I felt this calmness in my chest, and the rest of my body followed suit. I greeted them and went about my Father's business and read my poetry. Need I mention, this student body knew what it meant to be universal and accepting. They knew my friend was Muslim and allowed him to speak to the masses. There were hundreds of people there.

‖ PRESSPAUSE

This Christian journey has certainly taught me the meaning of humility, love, and acceptance. It has also taught me to forgive. But honey, the lessons I will not forget! I live in Rhode Island. The smallest state in the nation! I am bound to continue to run into these persons who have hurt me and made a significant impact in my life. I still greet them with a hug and smile. Not out of fakeness. But out of true love that Christ has deposited into my heart for them.

PASSION

What does the word *passion* mean to you? When I think of the word *passion*, I automatically see the word *red*. Red can be either a positive connotation or a negative connotation. It can be seen as anger, or it can be seen as eager excitement or love. I like to think of passion as a mixture of emotions that will provoke or prompt you to take action toward a goal or to protect. Café S.O.U.L. is my passion. At first, Café S.O.U.L. started as an idea for a solution to what I saw the city of Providence needed. As Café S.O.U.L. began to flourish, I started to become more and more passionate about the organization and what it stands for. The people's lives it started to positively impact. I allowed certain things to go undone and did not speak up when anything went against the vison and goal God gave me for Café S.O.U.L. but the passion within me brewed like coffee on a Sunday morning. Enough was enough, and I needed to speak up for myself and protect this vision!

We have a choice of what type of seed to sow. We have the opportunity to sow seeds that produce something that is everlasting. With that being said, if we sow a seed, it will be embedded in that person's life forever. Because seeds are deep-rooted, they will stay in that person's life. We can do something that will impact their life indelibly, whether good or bad.

Humility

Another lesson learned in this Christian walk in humility. What does humility look like? What does it mean to be humble as a Christian? I often had equated humbleness to meekness. I thought that I needed to always bite my tongue if I did not agree with something or if someone has offended me. Like Martin Luther King, turn the other cheek, and as the Bible scribes, how many times must we forgive those who have offended us? Seven times seven. But sometimes all that multiplication leads to a crescendo moment. You can only corner someone for so long before their inner lion or lioness lashes out.

➢ PRESSPLAY

Expectations (Realistic and Unrealistic)

As many people do, we can at times put unrealistic expectations on leaders and pastors. We can put them on pedestals that they do not belong on. Even if they put themselves there. We must start to lean in with curiosity and see them through a Christlike lens. See them as the imperfect humans that they are. Now, this does not give them license to be reckless. But this does grant them grace for things they have done imperfectly, knowingly and unknowingly. As mentioned previously, forgiveness is not for the other person but is for you. I would like to also add, that unforgiveness holds the person in the same spot where they committed an offense. Meaning, what if they have grown since the time, they have offended you. What if they now have a new insight and or belief and their actions back it up? Why must we hold them hostage to their old selves. Unforgiveness means that we are stuck in our pain and that means we are keeping them stuck in that same place. They may have grown or are growing, and we can't keep them in that same spot. Sometimes I wonder, at what point do we accept that "every saint has a past and every sinner has a future." When will we allow people to step into their destiny when we keep trying to make them walk in memory of their footsteps of the past?

When it comes to expectations, communication is key. Sometimes, what we think is obvious may not be as obvious to the other person. Like most relationships, needs and expectations must be communicated. This way, they know what is expected of them and can grant you their input if they can fulfill the expectation.

Another important factor is to evaluate our expectations. We shouldn't expect something from someone if we are not willing to do the same if we were in the position to fulfill it.

REFLECT

What are some of your expectations when it comes to church and the Christian body? Do you feel these are valid and realistic? Why or why not?

_____
_____
_____
_____
_____
_____
_____
_____
_____
_____
_____
_____
_____
_____
_____
_____
_____
_____
_____
_____
_____
_____

NEW BEGINNINGS

Church at Café S.O.U.L.? What?

August 2013, Cafe S.O.U.L. began hosting a church, and services were held at our location. Never in my life did I fathom such a possibility. At a time I was running away from church, church came running into me. The very vision that was deemed unorthodox and not Christlike was deemed the very place to congregate. The church congregation was very intimate. It was just what I needed to be reintroduced to be a member of a church body. I started to have a renewed relationship with God and His people. These were the steps I needed toward my healing.

Newfound Faith in Church

After a while, the pastor of the church held at Café S.O.U.L. needed a sabbatical. Being hungry for the Word and wanting fellowship, I reached out to a friend. She had been inviting me to come to her church for years. I was reluctant to go due to the previous relationships I encountered at churches. This was a big step for me. I decided to go and started to attend New Dimension Apostolic Center in January 2017. I then became a member and later became rebaptized in September 2017. New birth of new beginnings. I became a part of a larger church family again. I was able to trust again. Like any relationship, there is a level of trust that needs to develop. This starts with stepping outside of the hurt zone and making connections with the members at the church. This also grants an opportunity to redefine relationships.

So how do you start to find a new church after experiencing trauma? I first would start with prayer and seeing where God will lead you to join. Also, treat it like a job interview; while they may have questions at the church, you also come with your list of questions and expectations. Lay it all out on the table. Research about their mission and vision. Does it align with your values and beliefs? Also, set a foundation of how you would like to define your relationship with the church. Gain an understanding of what it is that they expect of you as a member of the church. Give them your expectations of what you expect of them as church leaders and the church body as a whole.

You never know, you may indeed find closure in another form. For me, that is true. Earlier in 2020, I let my pastor know about an accomplishment. She e-mailed me the simplest yet profound words: I AM PROUD OF YOU. Those few simple words hit me so hard. There was a visceral response, and all of a sudden, tears started flowing down my face and a deep cry released from my heart. It was like those were the words I needed to hear years ago from leaders.

I AM PROUD OF YOU that you reached your one-year anniversary for your business.

I AM PROUD OF YOU that you graduated with your master's in the midst of surviving a near fatal car accident and being let go from a job of six and a half years.

I AM PROUD OF YOU for seeing your worth and letting go of toxic relationships and friendships.

Yes, I received accolades from my mom, friends, and family. I am ever so grateful for their support. But, unconsciously, I also needed to hear that acknowledgement from my pastoral leaders.

Integrated Summaries

The next sections of this book, you will encounter real experiences of people I interviewed. These are very detailed experiences that may trigger some emotional memories or possible trauma that you may have endured yourself. This is a disclaimer to brace yourself for what you are about to read. If this causes any type of emotional or psychological warfare, I strongly encourage you to seek your therapist to work with what emotions or memories emerge. If you do not currently see a therapist, see your local directories for any clinicians in your area. I am a huge advocate of mental wellness and believe everyone has a story to tell and deserves to be healed and given the skills to cope with those traumatic experiences. This book has given people an opportunity to tell their story that they never had the chance to tell anyone. This gave them an opportunity to heal and release once and for all. It gave them the chance to forgive.

For the safety of the participants and to honor their identity, their names, as well as the names of family, friends, and organizations, are substituted with different names.

Rachelle's Journey

The case of Rachelle: Late bloomer Christian, my faith blossomed at the age eighteen. You can say I was a church nomad, going from one church to another. Because I began to lose hope in the people of God, never losing hope in God, I can't seem to find a church I can call HOME. Yes, I understand that we are imperfect. But why must I be cast out and feel as if I am not worthy to belong? My spirit has been crushed like a rose trampled on the road. Transparent moment: I was invited to a friend's church to minister through song. The church enjoyed my music ministry so much that they welcomed me on the worship family! I thought, finally, I can be a part of a church family! When I was comfortable enough to allow my guard down, I gave the worship team some tips and feedback. Like I said, they enjoyed my singing but did not want any parts of the leadership side of my anointing. Pinning back the wings of my potential, they met my feedback with snarky remarks, being very non-receptive.

One day, I was even allowed to prepare a solo piece for a special service which just so happened to be my birthday! I was so ecstatic and had been preparing for two weeks! The day of the event, I was asked by leadership what were my song selections. It just so happened that the song I chose was the same song the worship team was working on. You would think blessed minds think alike and we are in alignment, right? Unfortunately, that was not the case. Instead, I was ridiculed and yelled at to go back and pray to the Lord to download a new song into my spirit. They were more concerned about their shine being overshadowed than the true ultimate shine of the DIVINE. The petals of this flower were being plucked one by one; they like me, they like me NOT! I went to the back and created space in my heart for the Spirit to minister and give me peace. The Lord did give me a song that touched the entire congregation, to the point where the main pastor poured a prophetic word over me saying I would be leading a worship team of my own and he was going to ordain me a minister of music. Even the guest bishop said he would sow seed into my music ministry and invited me to come to his city and minister at his church; he would even fly me out there! As exciting as this was, there was an angst in my stomach. I couldn't even celebrate because I know that the worship team would be abhorrent of this vision. As I suspected, I was kicked off the worship team. That promised seed was misdirected to different soil.

At the same time all this complex yet beautiful disaster was occurring, I needed to move. Rather than support me in my efforts, the first lady started to pour shade over me, saying I left the church because I couldn't get money from the church and I left my husband to move to another city in a shelter. Let me tell you, when I ever stepped foot back into the church, the whispers of her false lies hovered in the sanctuary. That church treated me like I had an "S" on my chest, and it was not for super, but the mark of Scarlet—A. That was the last church "home" I have been to, and it has been eight years. When I left, no one reached out to me. REPLACEABLE. ANOTHER NUMBER. But I am not, because everyone has a unique anointing. That is why we need one another. We all complete each other in the body called church. To think that someone is replaceable is sad, but that is how it feels.

All I wanted to do and still do is to serve God, and well, that is still what I do. I travel and do what God has called ME to be, the church. We are the church wherever we go. I am at peace right now with my God and no longer have cares for the opinions and judgement of this world. I no longer carry baggage because that weighs me down while I am on this Christian walk and faith journey.

What it has taught me is how to love harder and practice what I preach. How to not be a hypocrite 101. "Jesus said to him, 'You shall love the Lord your God with all your heart, with all your soul, and with all your mind. This is the first and great commandment. And the second is like it: You shall love your neighbor as yourself.' On these two commandments hang all the Law and the Prophets'" (Matthew 22:37–40).

I know that not all Christians and churches are bad. I have experienced a church full of love and shown love from people of God. There is hope. I need to remind myself of who I am and Whose I am and not to lose sight of who I am just because of another person's actions.

REFLECT

_____
_____
_____
_____
_____
_____
_____
_____
_____
_____
_____
_____
_____
_____
_____
_____
_____
_____
_____
_____
_____

If you can relate, reflecting back on your current perspective, are you able to see through different lenses and perspectives? What would that look like? Jot it down below.

_____

_____

_____

_____

_____

_____

_____

_____

_____

_____

_____

_____

_____

_____

_____

_____

_____

_____

_____

_____

_____

_____

_____

_____

_____

_____

_____

_____

_____

Kennedy's Journey

Questions

The case of Kennedy: I have always had an insatiable curiosity about how things work, especially in life. Never taking things at face value. Everything in this world had a poker face, and I was determined to find what was the truth. Enamored from my first encounter with the Holy Spirit, I wanted to learn all I could know about Christ. Ushered to raise my hands high, head swayed back, and exclaiming Jesus over and over with tears of joy! It felt like I came from darkness to the light.

Distraction

There was this sly cat that called himself a youth pastor at the church I was attending. Not ordained and I am not sure if called at that time. I was all but thirteen years old, and he found it appropriate to talk about mostly sexual content. Not in an edifying, build-up-the-youth kind of talk. No! Disgusting rhetoric disguised behind manipulated scripture. He tried to satisfy his thirst by making a move on me. The only move made that day was me leaving that church. When I left the church, it sent me into a whirlwind of sin. Falling from grace, what some call backslidden. I took Christ out of my eyes and disassociated myself from Christ. It is one thing to disassociate yourself from church, but it is another thing to disassociate yourself with Christ. To me, you keep Christ in your heart, and He wasn't there anymore. I was mad.

Brokenhearted

Rather than following Christ, I followed the world. I mean, why break my neck to see sheep in wolves' clothing when I can see them selling the wolves' clothing and showing their real, true character. Hypocrisy at its best. Although I left Christ, He never left me.

What made me put Christ back into my heart and my eyes was the experience with the devil. It has always been said that this world is the devil's playground. But did you know that the devil comes dressed up in your flesh's desires? Tall and handsome, suited with a bowtie. I should have known this man was no good with that Cheshire cat from Alice in Wonderland smile. Oh, and he smelled so good. He had everything in the world but no soul. Red flags? I ignored them, including his fists. But like J LO, I eventually had enough! I called on the name of Jesus like the first time I caught the Holy Spirit and rebuked the demons out of that man! Literally! The power of Christ is REAL! People can argue the Bible all day, but they can never argue my experience with Christ.

Transformed

As the world kept attempting to debunk the truth of Christ, I kept searching for Him in the unlikely places. Who would have thought a two-dollar crucifix from a yard sale would have caused me to repent. Turning from my former life, God removed that abusive man from my life. I began to do my own thing, loving myself more, doing self-care before it was a trend. Started my own business, and that experience with the Holy Spirit as a young child stayed anchored in my soul. In need of navigating back to that younger part of me that believed and trusted, I started gaining my faith back. Once I got this power of doing me back, I came back to my senses. I had a story to tell! My heart's desire is to speak to the brokenhearted and lost. Although I have not been back to church, I still have a relationship with God. Because His Word is a bond, I vowed to never break this bond between Him and I. I have been on an amazing journey finding out who Christ is to me, and He is REAL! Glory be to God who sits on the throne above! I get excited!

Gem Drop

Words *Jesus Christ* has a meaning: *Jesus*—God is my salvation, *Christ*—spirituality and intellect.

My breakdown of who He is to me may sound different from what the church is telling me. I found out a lot greater information about who Christ is that the church fails to teach us.

REFLECT

What stood out to you in this vignette? In what ways can you relate? In what ways are you unable to relate?

If you can relate, reflecting back on your current perspective, are you able to see through different lenses and perspectives? What would that look like? Jot it down below.

_____

_____

_____

_____

_____

_____

_____

_____

_____

_____

_____

_____

_____

_____

_____

_____

_____

_____

_____

_____

_____

_____

_____

_____

_____

_____

_____

_____

_____

_____

Essence's Journey

The case of Essence: "Turch" was how I fashioned my lips to say the word church at a tender age of four. The torch of church was not automatically handed down to me. No. I had to actually beg my parents to bring me to church. That innocent desire and awe and wonder faded at the age of eight when I experienced something so devastating. So devastating that I cannot afford to unpack and undo all the hard work I have done in my adult years to tuck away the pain that turmoil caused me. That was just the proposition to more pain I had to endure spiritually and physically at home. Although my soul ached, I tried to join church again at the age of eighteen to escape my reality at home. However, I was met with the next level of agony as my character was assassinated by church members. I was talked down to, ridiculed, and cast aside. They made me feel like the heathen's they easily turned away from the church. Why couldn't anyone scoop me under their wing? Couldn't they see the painful environment I crawled out of? I don't need to be ostracized. I need to be nurtured and nourished with love.

This started to intensify the internal battle and turmoil. Reclusive was the lifestyle I adopted, since no one would adopt me. I would shy away from any kind of relationship to duck and dodge any notion of judgement. I mean, who wants to be friends with a heathen, right? I started to lose faith in humanity.

(Laughs to self.)

Press forward twenty years later, I can now look back and exclaim this has been a long voyage toward forgiveness. No easy feat! Navigating through various stages of coping. Initially, the instinct to cope was to stuff the pain deep within. Then, I began to harbor animosity toward the offenders. Bitter was the taste in my soul. Almost mustering enough courage to face the music and tell those offenders how horrible they were to me. Instead, I pivoted the other way and did not release my woe. Peace was not granted because I did not grant my voice to be heard. Gradually, along the span of seven years, I sat at the lap of my Daddy God and prayed, pouring out to Him all that tucked away hurt, shame, and guilt. What He offered was the greatest of healing which yielded for-giveness of those who trespassed against me. The most important relationship I needed all along was one with Abba Father.

New healthy relationships were able to be formed. Now adopted into a beautiful sisterhood, the Lord allowed me to be healed through the interwoven love from Him and these sisters, providing a secure chrysalis for me to develop and transition into the vibrant butterfly I am today.

REFLECT

What stood out to you in this vignette? In what ways can you relate? In what ways are you unable to relate?

_____

_____

_____

_____

_____

_____

_____

_____

_____

_____

_____

_____

_____

_____

_____

_____

_____

_____

_____

_____

_____

_____

_____

_____

If you can relate, reflecting back on your current perspective, are you able to see through different lenses and perspectives? What would that look like? Jot it down below.

_____

_____

_____

_____

_____

_____

_____

_____

_____

_____

_____

_____

_____

_____

_____

_____

_____

_____

_____

_____

Melissa's Journey

The case of Melissa: Though my father is a minister, my pain did not stem from his church, per se. Because, see, he was not the overseer of the church at the moment. The moment of time when I was with the father of my children. I would constantly try to get him to come to church. It was a battle that I could not seem to win. However, his mistress that he was seeing a few blocks up the street, around the corner, seemed to have won that battle instead. He lived with me for only three months and ended up getting hitched with her two weeks after he moved out. Then, that's when he decided to play father to her kids and husband to her and attend my church. Ha! The irony of it all, I tell you! My heart did not find the irony in it at all; it ached. I attempted to pour my concerns to the current pastor. Lo and behold, the mistress not only had ties to my now ex-boyfriend, she also had ties to the church. She was part of the church family, y'all! No exit interview given because the pastor swept it under the rug like broken glass. I gave myself my own exit and headed to the new church my father was overseeing, sensing it would be safer, and it was.

As I reflect back, because the situation was so easily overlooked, I didn't allow it to take hold of my heart and mind any longer. Besides, their marriage was not fruitful and did not last. Fourteen years will give you enough time to heal and reevaluate. A minister once fed my soul these simple words, "It will be okay." So I kept rehearsing it like the lines of a movie until it became a reality, and everything really was okay. Sometimes we have to allow ourselves to have childlike faith (**Matthew 18:2–4 | Childlike Faith**). Then we can easily believe that it is okay, and we can process that it is okay. If we do not allow the process, we ourselves will start to become devalued like what was swept under the rug. Now don't get me wrong, I just recently began this whole healing process. Because then, I devalued my healing by not dealing and coping with it then.

I did not allow myself to feel or express my pain or even allow myself to say what they did was wrong. What he did was wrong.

See, when I went to school as a child, "spare the rod, spoil the child" rings so very true at this present moment. Let us not think that we are too high and mighty to be disciplined. It does not matter how high you get, you still need to answer to God. My mistake was not so much seeing the red flags. It was seeing the inner spirit of that man and ignoring it purposely. A person's inner spirit permeates through their walk, talk, characteristics. Character. There is no need for titles because your inner spirit precedes you before you even speak honey!

REFLECT

What stood out to you in this vignette? In what ways can you relate? In what ways are you unable to relate?

_____

_____

_____

_____

_____

_____

_____

_____

_____

_____

_____

_____

_____

_____

_____

_____

_____

_____

_____

_____

If you can relate, reflecting back on your current perspective, are you able to see through different lenses and perspectives? What would that look like? Jot it down below.

_____

_____

_____

_____

_____

_____

_____

_____

_____

_____

_____

_____

_____

_____

_____

_____

_____

_____

_____

Ginnette's Journey

The case of Ginnette: As I reflect back like peeking in the rearview mirror, I view my experience as a positive experience. I must admit, in the beginning, the church and its leadership disappointed me. But now, I view them as humans with character flaws. We are all human. We all have flaws.

Maturation

Now that is not to say what was done was right. I had leaders who rejected me, making me feel the pressure to operate in my anointing over operating in my first ministry, my family. Did this make me bitter? Yes, initially. Over time, I invested my time in therapy, and with that time, I was able to have more compassion for others. This led me to a new ministry in healing others. This is where my strength comes from.

For self-compassion and self-care, I am not compelled to return to the church that caused the pain. Rather, I attend when I am Spirit-led only. The four walls of church no longer confine me. I am liberated because the church is me, and I love who I am. So if *me* is an alternative path, I'll take her. Some of my loved ones may be concerned. But I am at my happiest place. I've learned to do me and really love me.

Rejecting the dance of religion and embracing the intimate relationship with God. Living my life as BOLDLY and UNAPOLOGETICALLY AUTHENTIC as possible. Creating my own definition of happiness each day I awake and take a breath.

REFLECT

What stood out to you in this vignette? In what ways can you relate? In what ways are you unable to relate?

_____
_____
_____
_____
_____
_____
_____
_____
_____
_____

If you can relate, reflecting back on your current perspective, are you able to see through different lenses and perspectives? What would that look like? Jot it down below.

_____
_____
_____
_____
_____
_____
_____
_____
_____
_____
_____
_____
_____

Roseanne's Journey

The case of Rosanne: I was raised in church. I remember having such a hunger to become saved. Little did I know that hunger would be well-satiated with disappointment and control of my entire life. I wanted to be like my mom and be saved at a young age. The church had the women feeling like the only way you could be a successful woman was through marriage; hence, that became my life's ambition. #GOALS. Age seventeen, engaged to a young man I was dating for two years. Wedding bells that should have rang had clanged and dissipated. The day we were to exchange vows, he decided to take a bow out of my life. Devastated was I, wanting to commit suicide because I felt worthless and empty inside. I failed my church. Within months of March, I marched into a marriage with a different man that only lasted a week. WEAK, felt I. No, I can do this! Third time is the charm, right? Well, luckily it lasted for twenty-five years just to end in divorce.

> The definition of insanity is doing the same thing over and over again and expecting different results. (Albert Einstein)

This vicious cycle was all fueled by the incorrect teachings of the church I attended. My vision of success and love were tainted. These teachings literally had overridden my ability to think soberly or make rational decisions of what may seem obvious to others. I was so consumed with pleasing the church by obeying their rules and standards that has nothing to do with GOD! Their opinions weighed heavier to me, that they knew I loved God with all my heart. #Pedestal. All along, I could just love Him with my all and not have to please them. Because pleasing them was never enough.

This false illusion of success and judgement from the church caused me a lifelong pain. Pain that is so deep-rooted that it is indescribable. What's even more painful is when you express your pain caused by church, you are told to GET OVER IT! Get over it? Let it GO! Let it go? These unrealistic coping skills caused me not to deal with it at all. Just accept it, assuming this is my lot in life. But why? YES! Why me?

THE LIGHT

Shaking off the old identity not destined for me, I started to speak out. Making videos across multiple social media platforms. It was then, I finally blossomed with epiphanies and realizations. Both sad and liberating at the same time.

Most people would assume that it would be easy to get over church hurt or think that people need to take responsibility for their own actions. However, it is almost as similar as when people blurt out "Why doesn't she get out of that abusive relationship?" It is because their minds have been traumatized and taken captive. Words have power. When your worth is minimalized and you are mentally abused, you are not able to logically think in the same capacity you did before the encounter of the abusive relationship. Abuse is not only physical and verbal, it comes in many forms such as exertion of power like money.

Be a beacon of light in the world and do not judge others.

REFLECT

What stood out to you in this vignette? In what ways can you relate? In what ways are you unable to relate?

_____

_____

_____

_____

_____

_____

_____

_____

_____

_____

_____

_____

_____

_____

If you can relate, reflecting back on your current perspective, are you able to see through different lenses and perspectives? What would that look like? Jot it down below.

_____

_____

_____

_____

_____

_____

_____

_____

_____

_____

_____

_____

_____

_____

_____

_____

_____

Emily's Journey

The case of Emily: I don't want to sound like a broken record. But this record keeps getting played in several Christian women's lives. I, too, was in an abusive relationship as a young adult. I tried to seek guidance from my church leaders, but my situation was brushed away like a fly in the wind. An audacious statement was proclaimed that abusive relationships are just something women must endure in life. I vehemently disagree with that sentiment. The very statement has fueled my passion today to inform and educate young Christians about what God says in His Word about our daily lives. Do not be conformed to this world or to some misinformed concepts of religion from a male-dominated standpoint. I have decided to become not only a role model but an advocate for them. It pains me to my core to see generations upon generations of Christians who feel the church has trapped them in abusive, unloving, unfruitful relationships. I know you are thinking, "Well, they are free to choose, they chose those relationships themselves." Yes and no. See, when in a rigid religious church setting, perceptions and beliefs are shaped and molded by that church's doctrine which influences the choices that are made on a daily basis. These false teachings I encountered still impact me as an adult today. It has made me hypersensitive to perceived failure. For example, I divorced the abuser, and people still make snide remarks today, twenty years later! So I find myself tolerating more than I should from people and their behavior. This is in an effort not to be deemed as a relationship failure. In order to cope with the effect of past pain, I must constantly remind myself I am what God says I am. As a matter of fact, my grandfather used to say, "They talked about Jesus too," so this is nothing new. I intentionally and sometimes audibly speak encouraging words to myself. I immerse myself into the work I was called to do and ignore the rest.

Ironically, Matthew, the 18th chapter, talks about trying to go personally to resolve it one-on-one. If that doesn't work, arrange a meeting with the leaders; if that doesn't work, then the church should put such troublemakers—unrepentant people—out of the fellowship. Sometimes, some churches like the one I attended need to put their own selves out.

I can say I have grown a lot and embraced my calling of being a leader in the church. I hold that calling as one of the most important calls in my life, but I feel that same way for members who leave. I want to know why and is there anything the local church can do to help. Sometimes there's nothing that can be done; sometimes it's better for that person's soul to find another ministry, but the church should care if people leave and reach out to find out if there's anything that can be done to help.

REFLECT

What stood out to you in this vignette? In what ways can you relate? In what ways are you unable to relate?

_____

_____

_____

_____

_____

_____

_____

_____

_____

_____

_____

_____

_____

_____

_____

_____

_____

_____

_____

_____

If you can relate, reflecting back on your current perspective, are you able to see through different lenses and perspectives? What would that look like? Jot it down below.

_____

_____

_____

_____

_____

_____

_____

_____

_____

_____

_____

_____

_____

_____

_____

_____

_____

_____

Ashley's Journey

The case of Ashley: Raised in a Baptist church with several years of traumatic events that I wish not to bleed on this sheet of paper. But I will say that as of now, me and my household, we no longer attend church. It has been quite a few years. No, not because of so-called church hurt, per se. It was more so we can start our new journey, a new lineage.

Liberated generation.

Step back from churchanity and trace steps to pieces of me and have a REAL relationship with God. I visit a small congregation from time to time as they welcome me and my children with wide open arms of acceptance.

No judgement.

The pain we endured propelled us deeper into the embrace of God.

Faith stronger.

Health rejuvenated.

Reflect on the rigid traditional doctrine of man made me yearn deeper for the sweet wisdom and knowledge of God's REAL Word.

Still able to love.

Still able to share gifts.

Belly full of joy and Word.

May not be suitable for your woman of God label,

But I am suitable for the God I know and the God that knows me.

God's vindication for each occasion, the enemy caused calamity.

Recognize the hand of God is always on His children.

Causing enemies to stumble and suffer, reaping the very rotten seeds they sowed.

Enemies may have been relieved to rid my presence.

But little did they know,

His justice always prevails.

Going to therapy rescued me. I was nearing obesity at three hundred–plus pounds, eating my pain away. This was not the life I intended to live. Now, I learn to live for God and live for my children. The justice of the Lord…there is NOTHING like it! Vengeance truly is the Lord's, and I have been able to see in my lifetime his vindication. Reaping the bad seeds that they thought they could sow into this good soil. My soil rejects bad seeds with the covering and anointing over me and my family. Now those people who tried to hurt me and mine have to eat the rotten fruit from their harvest.

Rejection does not produce a bitter and angry crop for me. It has not caused me to fear to commit or love again. Instead, rejection has spun me into the arms of my Heavenly Father. Guiding me to rely on God MORE. To give MORE. Especially the mighty Word and gifts He has impregnated me with. Ha! I may not carry myself like a woman of God. But I know that I know God and HE knows ME!

Pain endured from church made my faith in God insatiable. Hunger to know the truth, I sought the LIGHT, which negated any and all manmade doctrines and traditions.

REFLECT

What stood out to you in this vignette? In what ways can you relate? In what ways are you unable to relate?

_____

_____

_____

_____

_____

_____

_____

_____

_____

_____

_____

_____

_____

_____

_____

_____

_____

_____

_____

If you can relate, reflecting back on your current perspective, are you able to see through different lenses and perspectives? What would that look like? Jot it down below.

_____

_____

_____

_____

_____

_____

_____

_____

_____

_____

_____

_____

_____

_____

_____

_____

Jonathan's Journey

The case of Jonathan: There was this cat that I knew. A person I called a friend and brother. He used to take me to church with him and his oh-so-religious mom and sister. I must say, they taught me a lot about God and the Bible and how to live righteously. One day, this cat was going on and on about how the devil was living and breathing in all my VHS tapes, cassette tapes, CDs, and especially my comic books. He told me I needed to purge myself and stop sinning by keeping these devilish things around me and in my home. He went on and on about how I should throw them out. Because I trusted him, I ended up believing him. He helped me bag them in a big trash bag and take them to the dumpster. We talked some more and then he decided to head home to another part of town. As I peeked through my third-floor window, I noticed this cat hopped in the trash dumpster, find my bag of "demonic" items, throw them over his shoulder, and head home. Needless to say, I lost faith in a lot of things that day.

> Why do you look at the speck of sawdust in your brother's eye and pay no attention to the plank in your own eye? MATTHEW 7:3

The above vignette was just a small sample of the scenario that occurred. I did not have the opportunity to ask what happened after that point. I don't know if he ever confronted the guy or just altogether ended all contact with him. There are two ways this can be seen, depending on experiences and perspectives. On one side, some would say the guy took the CDs for himself and on the other side, some people can say that he took the CDs in order to avoid "temptation" of his friend to go back and get the CDs. My concern here goes deeper than that. Where is the ability to teach about the relationship with Christ come in? Where does this purging of evils come from? I know there are a number of scriptures that can be used for both perspectives. These days, you have to break it down for people. Don't just go purging their treasured items without truly going into detail. Also, what causes one to sin does not necessarily cause another person to sin. Personally, at this time of my life, I can listen to certain songs, and it does not cause me to want to sin. I do think whether Christian or any other walk of life, it is imperative to be mindful of what we are feeding our Spirit and our mind. Rather than listen to negative lyrics, listen to songs that encourage and uplift. The music genre can range from being Christian or another faith to, YES, even secular. I personally enjoy listening to artists like India Arie and Jill Scott. We must plant the seeds of wisdom and allow the person time to make the decision. Allow God to send people along the way to help with the cutting of the weeds and watering of the seeds. This day and age, people want not just authenticity but also practicality. Break it down, not water it down, but make it applicable to their life. Just like clients for therapy, the interaction is not cookie cutter. It is uniquely tailored and created in each encounter.

What are your personal thoughts of the above vignette? Write your reflection(s) below.

_____

_____

_____

_____

_____

_____

_____

_____

_____

_____

_____

_____

_____

_____

_____

_____

_____

_____

_____

   If you can relate, reflecting back on your current perspective, are you able to see through different lenses and perspectives? What would that look like? Jot it down below.

_____

_____

_____

_____

_____

_____

_____

_____

_____

_____

_____

_____

_____

_____

_____

_____

_____

_____

Malinda's Journey

The case of Malinda: When I was a little girl, my grand-mom used to infrequently take me to church, when she could spare time like change. By the time I was seventeen, I noticed my brother was going to church all the time. I was in awe and curious to know what was at this church that intrigued him. I decided to go and everything changed! The youth church pastor was awesome! I joined the choir and every other ministry I could get into and was there every Sunday! It was at this church that my passion grew for Christ. Now, I cannot paint a picture of all roses and not acknowledge the few thorns along the way. As I got older, as most Christian women pray for, I met my husband at church. He was handsome and an up-and-coming pastor. These characteristics caused me to look past the red flags. Although I was a pastor's wife in public, I was married to an abusive man behind cold, closed doors. His behavior at church was one way, and his behavior at home was different. This caused my trust in men and people to plummet. This experience was very confusing. It was scary. There was a period where there was a lot of discomfort because he was a pastor and we were going through the divorce and the church blamed me. He would leave it open on the pulpit for interpretation to lead them to believe the cause of divorce was me.

Separated.

Alone.

Ostracized.

Ashamed.

There was no longer any comfort in the church.

This marriage was new and this was my first experience in marriage. I felt so alone, so I started to seek healing elsewhere. That started a cycle of relationships I should not have been in. Meeting the wrong people, I was very defensive to protect myself around men I met. It was due to anxiety and PSTD, repeated cycles of abuse.

I am at peace and have outgrown that season.

I took the time to heal and redevelop my relationship with God. It brought me closer to Him. My distrust with people originally affected my relationship with Him. I rebuilt trust in the Lord.

I began to read the scripture more. Pray more. Recommitted myself to church. I sat down and reflected on myself, my life because I had to take responsibility as well. Reevaluation and taking time to get closer to God. I was feeding my Spirit with books from T. D. Jakes and Creflo Dollar. It is like a relationship, I had to be intentional and creative in regaining my faith.

Be a beacon of light in the world and do not judge others.

REFLECT

What stood out to you in this vignette? In what ways can you relate? In what ways are you unable to relate?

_____
_____
_____
_____
_____
_____
_____
_____

_____

_____

_____

_____

_____

_____

_____

_____

_____

    If you can relate, reflecting back on your current perspective, are you able to see through different lenses and perspectives? What would that look like? Jot it down below.

_____

_____

_____

_____

_____

_____

_____

_____

_____

_____

_____

_____

_____

_____

_____

_____

_____

_____

_____

Sasha's Journey

The case of Sasha: For me, growing up in a black church was disastrous. I grew up in black church, Ebenezer Baptist, one of the largest black churches in Rhode Island. Fairly large girl population, in which majority of them were fast. Always interested in boys. As for me, I was not interested in chasing boys. I was too concerned about academics and getting the best grades and excelling in school. Later, I started working and met with a few bad people. I mean, the worst that this state has to offer, one of which is in jail for murder, who chopped up a woman and dumped her in the dumpster. Regardless of their crime, I accepted them for who they were. Church is supposed to take everyone in, as we should, because we are to be a forgiving place. Unfortunately, I found out it was not forgiving. Picture this, the judgement in the church was so bad, it got to the point where young girls in the church who got pregnant ended up leaving the state.

My side of the story: As I said earlier, I was not interested in chasing boys. I was interested in men. I ended up talking to a bad dude; he was in his late twenties, and I was only fifteen. I was going out with him and thought it was cool. I didn't know or understand that what he was doing was considered statutory rape. This guy would give me alcohol. I never took drugs. Just wasn't my thing to do drugs. One night, I was super excited! SENIOR PROM! My mom allowed me to use her new car to ride in style to Venus de Milo for senior prom. The dude I was dating at the time asked me to leave the prom as he hadn't seen me and wanted to give me a present. I was excited and was ignorant at the time, so naive. I went by his house. The last thing I remember was drinking what I thought was a rum and coke. I just remembered being dragged down the stairs and nothing else I can remember. I woke up about an hour later and slipped on my prom dress and left. The next day, I was very campy and sick. I can recall fragmented pieces, seeing images of a man that was not my boyfriend at the time. I was perplexed. So I called him, and he didn't pick up. I looked in my purse and all my personal things were gone. I was able to finally get a hold of him a week later, and his snarky reply was, "I didn't do anything to do you, you had sex with me and my boy." While I am experiencing emotions and am STARTLED, FROZEN IN SHOCK, he started becoming belligerent and called me a whore and a slut.

The Church: Four months from the incident, I was very sick, and I found out I was pregnant. The church was mad, not mad at me, but mad I would not let them know what happened. So they threw me out. OUTCAST. Sad thing is, I was much more concerned about what they would have thought about the dumb mistake I made to leave to go to his house. I'd rather have them think I was a whore than to let them know I was assaulted. Got the name of his "boy," my father looked him up, went to his father, and his father's nonchalant reply was "He is a grown adult, you have to deal with him." Thoughts just kept racing through my mind. Do I keep her or not? You never know what decision to make until you are in that abortion room. Because of my medical condition, I could not abort the child, as I am considered a high risk. Still would be considered a high risk until this day. My family was against me having the abortion, and my father wanted me to keep it. Therefore, I decided to have the child. Humph! The church felt I had shamed them and the family.

Angry and sad, I attempted to commit suicide twice. My parents were so ashamed and switched congregations.

Two of the former deacons would come by and check in on me. The head pastor never came to visit, and the pastor's wife would roll her eyes and suck her teeth whenever she saw me. She thought less of me, looked down on me, and judged me. These were people I was to confide in. I don't know what to do or who to talk to. HURT. REJECTED. I decided to just leave the church, and I worked two jobs.

I had another pastor who came and check in on me who tried to come to me to come back to Ebenezer church. I wasn't trying to hear it. I silently asked myself, "Why are they really here?" as they asked a list of questions about my life like why do I have to work three jobs. Maybe they didn't know that I need to also keep my mind off my traumatic experience of rape. I constantly have to ask myself why I was assaulted.

The world: I met up with a group of women who were prostitutes and Wiccan. I joined the Wiccan faith. Honestly, it was a lot more welcoming than what people thought. They said, "We understand your situation, and you are welcome, and everything will be just fine." They then introduced me to someone who allowed me to live with them rent-free. He just required me to get my act together. I tried the best that I could. I was house-bouncing for over a year and half. I was homeless. Back at that church, they were still talking junk about me. How are all these alleged Christians around me not being Christian? The ones I am to come to confide in are gossiping, the same thing people do in the world, while you have the Bible in your hand, singing hymns. The tea and the huge hat mentality do not work. Stop spilling the tea because the dress-up is all just pomp and circumstance. I was so angry and ready to fight the pastor's wife. The woman ended up excusing herself from church when she saw me arrive. She is now a part of the head of the church in question, Ebenezer church. How is it that the world embraces me more openly than my childhood church?

As time went on, I entered graduate school and joined a new church body. My current pastor attended my master's graduation. There was a couple that had passed by and asked, "Don't I know you from somewhere?" FROZEN. LOST FOR WORDS. I just stood there and was like, "You can't be serious!" I wanted to tell them, "You people destroyed me and my family and my faith in Christ and all of a sudden you have no idea who I am?" It was the pastor and his wife. Not going to take my sunshine away! My current pastor was rooting for me in my accomplishments. I looked back to them and calmly said, "I am not sure who you are."

Moral of my story: Your position with God does not define your faith. It is your actions that determine your faith. Always remain the beacon of light in the world and do not judge others.

REFLECT

What stood out to you in this vignette? In what ways can you relate? In what ways are you unable to relate?

_____

_____

_____

_____

_____

_____

_____

_____

_____

_____

_____

_____

_____

_____

_____

_____

_____

_____

_____

If you can relate, reflecting back on your current perspective, are you able to see through different lenses and perspectives? What would that look like? Jot it down below.

_____
_____
_____
_____
_____
_____
_____
_____
_____
_____
_____
_____
_____
_____
_____
_____
_____
_____
_____
_____
_____
_____
_____
_____
_____
_____
_____
_____
_____
_____
_____

Julian's Journey

The case of Julian: I will be honest, I was debating on whether I truly wanted to dig back in that bag of pain, frustration, and confusion. But after seeing and witnessing the overall downfall of mankind and the so-called impact the church implies, I feel it's only right and extremely necessary to expose the pain and consistent misguidance of people who so desperately want and need answers. I'm tired of the church and their implication that it has the answers and that it is filled with flawed people yet they believe they are above the very people they're sent to help. So yes, I will answer your questions, I will help because I TRULY love everyone. I TRULY want to see ALL—black, white, gay, whoever, whomever—happy and excited about this gift we've been bestowed called life! Thank you for sharing and granting people the ability to share their stories as well. I think this is an amazing project, and so many people will be transformed through it. These questions really made me think about what I went through.

My story is a little complicated. My mother was raised in the church, and I also was raised in the church. When we were younger, we went with my grandmother, and we went to different churches—Baptist, Pentecostal, etc. While my father's side were Jehovah's Witness. We started going when I was seven years old. It was at first just me and my sisters. We built a relationship with the church, enjoyed going to Sunday school, sang in the choir, and were at awe when we saw people catch the Spirit. It was more of an activity to do on Sundays. Mom was doing her own thing. It was always fun and rewarding to go to church as a child. However, as we matured, we realized more. Things were more salient. The church was still a family church; everyone was related from pastors to Sunday school teachers. The church started to be like a family. Mom even started to go to church! We didn't have a car, it was cold, and we would walk. In the winter. Sometimes they would give us a ride, but most of the time, we walked. Now thinking back, I ask why had no one ever asked to give us a ride? Why was it not consistent? You see a single mother with six kids, and no one thought to pick us up and drop us off?

EXPECTATIONS

As I got older, I developed a deeper relationship with the church. As I began to trust them, I became more involved in a lot of ministries such as a helper, children's ministry, worship ministry with the lyric projections, developed a relationship with the pastor's daughter and her fiancé at the time, they were my go-to people. There was a point in my life when I went to college and became rebellious and partied and drank and lost sight of the disciplined identity which was not my identity in college. I wanted to do what *I* wanted to do. I left college and had a roommate, and the church did everything they did to recruit me because I had backslidden.

BACKSLIDDEN

Church was my life. I went to church every day. I just needed a break. I recall one night particularly, and the pastor's daughter and fiancé said they wanted to help me get back on my feet, get back into the church. I had a party and invited them because I felt I needed their guidance; they slowly but surely came to the party, and I was drunk. I felt guilty, and the pastor's kid was there. I remember a few weeks later, I decided to move out and get my life on a different path, and it really created a big to-do with my friends at that point. People said I thought I was trying to be better, I was so gung ho to get back on my feet. I moved into a studio downtown Newport that I could not afford but needed to be on my own to create a new path. I only was there for a month, and I was blessed to move into subsidized housing. I then heavily started going back to church, the teen ministry, mentorship within the teen ministry. I started to influence my sisters and my cousin to attend church. A lot of the neighborhood teens that knew me started to attend also. Being involved again really did help me get back on track, but there was a level of pretentiousness where we were not allowed to share our lives.

Kids had to throw away their worldly CDs and DVDs and had to throw them in a circle and burn them. I felt it was over the top. I didn't throw my CDs and DVDs in there. The daughter's fiancé would help me study right after he got out of work, ten o'clock at night, to prepare me for my SATs. They invested in me, helped me get material for college. I built such a strong bond with them, they invested in me. Fast forward, I felt indebted to them and respected them so much and wanted to do whatever to be in their good graces. They were like a big brother and big sister to me; I wanted to be like them. I was the oldest, and everyone looked up to me. I never had a big brother or big sister I could look up to and confide in.

There was a point where I wanted to sing. I sung, and they turned it down and said I needed to get lessons. To me, the church always wants us to use their gift, but when we bring up our interest, there is nothing there to help develop the gift in the church. So we go outside, and we end up in the secular world. They expect their gift to be tiptop or else it's not their calling, according to the church. I felt like, WOW, I am finally a part of something.

ACCEPTANCE

There was a young man I mentored, and I would meet him on Wednesday evenings at church. He was considered a troubled teen. I took it upon myself and asked his mother if I could mentor him. Thursday evenings, we would spend time watching movies. There was a point he was so rebellious, his mom couldn't take it anymore, so I moved him in. I felt I had something to offer to mentor. I know I was only twenty-three and he was sixteen, but I was confident that I could help him. I went through a lot of struggles and I had crutches and I was still supporting him. My mentor admired what I was doing. Eventually, we started to clash, the young man and I, because I am a very direct no-take-mess type of person. Then he and his family would disrespect me and then he started to run away. We had a big falling out, and he moved out to go back to live with his mother. One day, we were at church, and he busted into church and he was yelling and screaming right before worship started. He was beaten up badly. My mentee thought I had something to do with him getting beat up. I was then pulled into the pastor's office and was told that I was too young to take in the young man.

JUDGEMENT

However, everyone in the church saw his struggle and did not do anything to help monetarily, go to his school to meet with the teachers and principal, help him to study, or use their energy, time, and resources. I was on crutches taking the bus going to these meetings. All these grown men in the church who had the ability and resources did nothing to help this sixteen-year-old. Yet I am being told I should never have done it. I helped made progress in his life. He still, until this very day, calls me and asks me ten-plus years later to mentor him, to ask big life questions, and to thank me for being active in his life and never giving up on him. But the church didn't. Nonetheless, at that time, I started to think, maybe I am not cut out for the teen ministry or this church thing. It started to bore me, and everything was the same, the songs, the sermon topics, etc. In the meantime, I published a book, and I was very active in the community. I was invited to speak at a domestic abuse vigil from another church and read a poem from my book. I never was invited from my church to speak about important topics and my book. My pastor at the time attended the vigil. I was still very invested in my church tithing, at the same time as traveling around with my book for book releases. There came a point where I knew I needed a change in my life. At the same time of my need for transition, my big brother and big sister tied the knot.

ABANDONED

I felt like I was losing them, people I could confide in. I know that isn't true, but that's how I felt. I was tired of passing flyers around the city that God loves you. I wanted to make real impact and change in the community. I then went to talk to my spiritual brother and sister, and she was about to give birth. I wanted to leave the youth ministry. I could not meet with them because they were busy with life and expecting the baby. I also, though not physically pregnant, was pregnant with ideas and a purpose that required change and guidance. What I was personally able to do was to be bigger than the church. I was pressed. I was very open and honest and transparent. I am not fake and that is not my story. I am not going to tell these kids one thing and then the next thing I am telling them other. I had to avoid a lot of the kids' questions and send the kids of other people. I know these pastors have a story, and they are choosing to hide it and only show their perfect side. Finally, I met with my spiritual brothers and sisters and the meeting of minds became a clash of personas. He could tell I was just going through the motions. We then ended on a decent note of it being a perfect time to transition; the next ministry meeting. I built deep relationships with these kids. I was NOT allowed to tell the kids I was leaving. As I was leaving, there was no wish you well, no thank you for your services, all the youth leaders went upstairs. I was by myself, and I just left. That was the close of it. I felt alone and betrayed. IT WAS COLD. After everything I gave to this church, this ministry!

After that, my relationship with all the youth leaders changed; they treated me differently. I was good when I was in it but not good enough when I am ready to do something bigger and greater that was best for me in that season. After this, everything I was doing in college got magnified times ten. I was like a kid kicked out of his parent's house. So I spiraled and did everything I could to get attention. The Parable of the Lost Son was no longer a parody as Luke 15:11–32 started to draw a reality in my life.

After leaving the church and having a good ol' time, I still went to church, but it wasn't the same. My relationship changed. How is it you can invest all your life, resources, energy to church and decide you want to go a different direction, the church is so comfortable to easily disown you? How can they be totally okay with that? No blessing? How can they call themselves a minster or pastor and not totally operate in that FULLY? I understand that we are human beings. A lot of people get comfortable in their titles and forget who they are. I was HURT by that. I was hurt by people whom I thought were my family. I invested so much of myself. They invested in me as well, but I would have never done what they did. I would not allow someone to just walk away and not thank them or celebrate them. My life spiraled from that point because the relationship that I was taught to build was a relationship with people and not spiritual. When everything fell, EVERYTHING fell. I knew what I experienced, and I was not allowed to say anything. I was not allowed to speak my truth because they didn't want me to influence them. We had to be pretentious to keep them for bodies, for numbers. How can we relate to these kids in this time and era? We must be able to connect on some level.

That day, THAT DAY when I left the ministry was so hard for me. Even if the other youth leaders felt some type of way, my spiritual big brother and big sister should have reached out to me.

REVELATION

I was in an adult store, I recognized the face and realized it was one of the pastors in my church. I was BLOWN AWAY by that. Not so much that he was there, but it was so much a facade being put on. I go to church the next Sunday, and he gives his speech and rant right before the congregation about something that does not follow. Him and his wife were counseling my aunt and boyfriend on how they should live and not live, but they are a higher up elder doing the exact opposite of what was coming out of their mouth. You pretentiously preached to my family that they were not good enough and lived in sin, but YOU were just in an adult store without your wife and ONLY I knew the truth.

I told my spiritual mentor about the situation; her response was what if that is his struggle. But that same grace was never granted to me. It's so FAKE. I was done; hypocrisy in the church was real, and I could not take it. My attendance in church concluded in 2009. Until this day, I still do not attend church. I will not be affiliated with contradiction. I have forgiven them. I am truly free and have no remorse. I am confident in my identity.

My Gripe/My Vent

They don't check up on you or send a message or card. The address is used for tax purposes to send your tithes. They do not show up or call just to check in on you. You don't get that until you show up and throw a little offering in the collection plate. Don't you have my address? My phone numbers?

Relationships change, and people can get caught up in their own life and egos. Good and bad. What does that do for that individual? Have you made the person you are guiding strong or are you continuing to contribute to their pain, hurt, and weakness?

There will be times when you will fail or feel like you are falling and failing. You must be strong enough to handle both.

We love ourselves in these RELIGIOUS relationships

I believe spirituality is too big of a subject to put into one religion. I do not associate with any religion; I will never. I respect religious beliefs. My personal everyday belief: I identify myself as spiritual, align myself with the person's positive spiritual vibes. The church is to be a hospital, but when you go into the hospital, you don't get healed. You come out with a Band-Aid. That's not healing; the wound is open and live. A lot of times, the church was instrumental to the cause of that wound. I have always dealt with rejection. The church where I am supposed to come to with open arms rejected me. I reached out and there was minimal male involvement in the church.

You cannot truly help someone if you are not transparent

I believe in THOROUGH transparency. If you are going to preach and inspire, preach from the heart and what is relative. Like in school, some teachers assume all students learn the same way. How many students do you miss with that approach? Same for church, how many people are you missing with your message? It is way more helpful and inspiring with transparency. It is way more helpful for when that person leaves church and goes home. They are uplifted to handle real life situations.

You don't have to look and smell a certain way

Just because you are a pastor or leader does not mean you do not struggle; your title does not mean that much, that you are better or in a higher place. Why can't you share your story when you are doing the same thing I am? Why not inspire me rather than ridicule me for what you are going through? We are both backslidden as you would say.

I would be thorough

Not sit around and gossip. Not holding back how you feel. Take off your religious hats and titles and TALK and ENGAGE. Be a spiritual individual and understand the emotion that they are experiencing. Find out and come to an agreement or agree to disagree. NEVER allow a person to walk away because your position and your ego won't allow you to apologize.

Churches can thrive

Family-ran churches has bias. Are you really going to tell your daughter or son-in-law that they are wrong? Are they going to receive the same disciplinary action or judgement? POLISHED.

Some churches thrive from popularity and competition. That disgusts me. If you are about winning and helping souls, then help them to be better here on earth; competition should not be a motive.

Churches die for various reasons. There is so much to both sides. Die due to being mundane. As human beings, our attention span gets bored. Money is a huge thing in church. Buy million-dollar buildings within the same community that has homelessness. Is it a church or a music theatre? Is it a church or a concert hall? You say people should not come to church for entertainment, but you are making it an entertainment like Gillette Stadium. CONTRADICTORY. You are providing the entertainment. Antics, jumping, hooting, and hollering. That takes away from the message.

PASSION: I have no interest in renewing my passion for the church. Don't have a passion for the building. It's the people you should have passion for. Your spiritual being is all I am concerned about. We are all spiritual beings. Even agnostic persons who do not want to acknowledge they are spiritual beings. That's how we connect, by the Spirit. How I contribute is by publishing books and giving them an outlet to release that. They are also granting others to do the same. Renew your passion by finding out your purpose. Not for the church, the mundane religiosity of what goes on within the four walls of the church. Because all things can change, but does your spiritual identity change? Do you HAVE a spiritual identity? A church can benefit from reevaluation. Are you, as a church, concerned about their spiritual well-being? Or are you concerned about the external factors of which can be judged? Your focus should be to develop their spiritual identity.

A church is not the end all, be all. Just like a car. A car can drive anywhere in the continent in the US. Is that to say only one gas station has the ability to fuel my tank? We are spiritual beings that can traverse anywhere in this world. I need the gas to get to the next city or state.

REFLECT

What stood out to you in this vignette? In what ways can you relate? In what ways are you unable to relate?

_____
_____
_____
_____
_____
_____
_____

_____

_____

_____

_____

_____

_____

_____

If you can relate, reflecting back on your current perspective, are you able to see through different lenses and perspectives? What would that look like? Jot it down below.

_____

_____

_____

_____

_____

_____

_____

_____

_____

_____

_____

_____

_____

_____

_____

_____

_____

ॐ

"Natural Pearls
form when an irritant—
usually a parasite and
not the proverbial grain
of sand—works its way
into an oyster, mussel,
or clam. As a defense
mechanism, a fluid is
used to coat the irritant.
Layer upon layer of
this coating, called
nacre, is deposited
until a lustrous
pearl is formed."

—Countess B.

ॐ

MATURATION
AND GROWTH

Upon the completion of each interview, there were a few questions that were asked about in what ways we can improve as Christians in our own walk. Below are responses. I also invite you to write, reflect, and write down any ways you believe you can become a better follower of Christ and how we can do better as the body of Christ.

1. WHAT WOULD YOU HAVE DONE DIFFERENTLY IN YOUR SITUATION IF YOU WERE THE OTHER PERSON(S)?
   - Do the exact opposite of what they did to me. Allowing someone to vet or vent. Allowing someone to help develop a plan. I ended up going into a welfare office and the caseworker said, "I can get you welfare and section 8, but I have a feeling that this is not for you." You would have to go to a single-parent nunnery, and they would allow me to get my act together. I chose the latter, the nunnery, and got my act together. I would like the church member and Christian friends and families to show me alternatives and an action plan or option. Tell me like it is but then assist me with a resolution.
   - If I were the pastor, I would have gotten together with the hurt individual first to see what the root cause of hurt is. Then I would have brought all of us together and then try to figure out the root of the problem. "How can we resolve this and how can we heal this situation?"
   - Pray on it, cry, work with me on a plan like the caseworker did.
   - Seek therapy and go to the root of the problem.

- Definitely reach out to the individual and see if there is anything that could be worked out. Whatever the issues are, I would make sure that I try my best to resolve or provide a solution.
- I would be more helpful. Listen and ask the right questions without being nosy and genuinely help and pray.
- I would have prayed and encouraged the other person rather than implying they were a failure because they did not want to tolerate abuse.
- I would have preached and become focused on saving souls. I would have used the platform of the youth ministry for the purpose of guiding them spiritually.
- I would have talked and communicated rather than lashing out. I feel like people have a hard time being honest and real. Especially persons in leadership. I feel like they put on a front to be strong, but we also need to see that they are a real person and that they go through things too or struggle. Open up about feelings to have a better understanding of feelings. Or reach out once I saw the person was no longer there. When I left the church, no one reached out to me to see how I am doing.

REFLECT

_____

_____

_____

_____

_____

_____

_____

_____

_____

_____

_____

_____

_____

_____

_____

_____

_____

_____

_____

_____

_____

_____

2. HOW SHOULD CONFLICT IN THE CHURCH BE HANDLED?
    *   By having an open line of communication.
    *   In a conflict, if it deals with emotions, people need to take a step back before they say and do anything that they will regret. Do not provide feedback while in emotions like anger. Sometimes it takes a day or weeks, whatever time it takes to allow people to work out their negativity and emotions. Does not mean to wait twenty to thirty years because you are hiding from conflict.
    *   Seek healing as soon as possible when it comes to human relationships. If not handled as soon as possible, it can manifest to something negative in all aspects of life that deal with relationship.
    *   If you see something in church that is not right, stand up for that person or persons and support them.
    *   Much prayer and much understanding and empathy. Be non-judgmental. Simply take the time to listen.

- I think it's important that leaders are trained, educated, and capable of speaking to people with grace, love, and compassion. I think it is the local church's responsibility to teach the truth found in God's Word and not *their* truth. I think conflict should be resolved immediately as to allow it to linger only causes things to fester.
- Openly. Honestly. I don't think it's a good idea to cover up stuff that goes on in church. I also don't think that the church should HIDE when leaders fall. LET the world see them fall! Let the people see them fall! RESTORE THEM. LOVE them. Be patient and loving with them. Throw NO ONE away. THIS is why leaders do what they do and why suicide and depression among church leaders is SO high. There is no safe place for leaders to go when they mess up. And they WILL!
- Conflict in the church should be handled with care and compassion because mental heal issues are running rampant in all communities.
- I think it depends on what are the conflicts. Case-by-case scenarios depend on who and what it is. Some people would need a meeting or prayer or knowledge. Some people are not aware, so knowledge is a powerful piece. Some people do not care, and so then you need to pray for them. There is not one solution. Everyone is different. If you did one thing for everyone, the people may not be able to get where they need to be as far as for healing and closure.
- At all costs, conflict should be confronted with prayer and discussion between the concerned individuals. If the conflict persists, then with appropriate counsel and all involved parties present. Hopefully, bringing the conflict to light will bring about some resolution. It's biblical: Matthew 18:15–17 says, "If your brother sins against

you, go and tell him his fault, between you and him alone. If he listens to you, you have gained a brother. But if he does not listen, take one or two or three witnesses. If he refuses to listen to them, tell it to the church."

- Have the conflicted parties sit together in front of leadership or the pastor and express what is going on. Let's nip it in the bud and get it off your chest. Judgement-free zone. Church persons tend to not come to each other and communicate to each other what is on their chest because they are fearful of being judged or they are the one's judging.
- If you have an issue, go to the person. If that does not work, then bring someone with you as a witness, and if that does not work, then bring it up to leadership and try to have everyone sit down.

If therefore you are offering your gift at the altar, and there remember that your brother has anything against you, leave your gift there before the altar and go your way. First be reconciled to your brother, and then come and offer your gift. (**Matthew 5:23–24**)

- There was a man who came to a previous church I attended. He was a pastor and came to preach. It was not known what happened, but the church kicked him out of church and said that the man and his family and kids could never come back to the church. Excommunication. I was like, can that happen? If someone is involved in ministry, there needs to be a conversation and a plan to trigger the root problem. Advise the person to take a step back to concentrate and resolve the issue. I do not think that excommunication should happen. Who are we to deny Christ because of their personal problems or issues? If they are not able to resolve the issues, then they cannot serve and need more help to resolve their issues.

REFLECT

_____

_____

_____

_____

_____

_____

_____

_____

_____

_____

_____

_____

_____

_____

_____

_____

_____

_____

_____

_____

3. WHEN IS IT RIGHT TO LEAVE A CHURCH?
   - When GOD says to GO. Period. You will know.
   - When it is messing with your faith, it is time to go. There is no reason whatsoever that any human being should be messing with your faith.
   - When the Spirit of the Lord commands you to do so.
   - When your heart tells you to leave, then it is time.
   - When you no longer gain any spiritual value from the church.

- To me, I don't know if there is a right or wrong time. I think you should be led. If you feel you are spiritually dying or not growing or the teaching is not correct and not biblically sound doctrine, you want to go to the church that is biblically sound and with love. It is all about loving.
- I feel it's time to leave the church when YOU are ready to leave. As humans, we know when something is not right. Sometimes we use, "I am waiting for God to release me," out of fear. You really think God wants you to wait five to ten years to continue to go through the church hurt and pain you are going through? We have our own time clock within. The pastor is not God. These human relationships we make we substitute the spiritual connection. I don't need your permission.
- I believe that it's right to leave the church when you are being led by the Spirit of God or if you feel that you are being used or mistreated.
- When God tells you. Because you are going to be hurt everywhere. Hurt should not be the reason why you leave a church. There may be a motivation behind the hurt, but there is no perfect church. God has lessons for us daily, and sometimes the lesson is in our pain. He could be teaching us to be and who not to be. We need to open our minds to what He has for us.
- It's right to leave a church at any point. Knowing what your own spiritual needs are helps to be able to gauge whether you are getting spiritually filled or not. If you're feeling uncomfortable, stifled, disconnected, judged, ostracized, or WHATEVER, we were given free will, by all means, it's fine to move on. One should not be made to feel that they are to remain in a state of discomfort at all.
- When you don't feel spiritual growth. It is nice to see the people, but if I don't get the Spirit from the pastor when

they talk or speak the Word there is no spiritual nour-ishment. I listen very closely. I need spiritual uplifting. I love a good sermon. I like the old church music; it had more Spirit in it. I don't really like the new contemporary songs. I want to hear someone who has got soul.

- When you are not getting what you need and, more importantly, not able to give to it your gifts. If I walk out the same way I walked in Sunday after Sunday and I do not feel different or a change, I am not able to serve with what gift God gave me, then it is time to go. If things I brought to the attention to the pastor is not being acknowledged or fixed over and over, then it is time to go.

REFLECT

_____
_____
_____
_____
_____
_____
_____
_____
_____
_____
_____
_____
_____
_____
_____
_____
_____

_____

_____

_____

_____

_____

_____

_____

_____

_____

4. WHY DO SOME CHURCHES THRIVE WHILE OTHERS DIE?
- One of the most unanswerable question, as a whole, people have had enough. Monetarily, when you can't even make ends meet yourself; mentally, not emotionally not speaking to you and to today's issues, with the word. Negativity in a church can cause a church shutdown. Physically fighting with fist in front of church members.
- It depends on who wants to sell their soul out the most. Nowadays, leaders are making deals with the devil just to have the most recognized church. By being recognized, that means you have you more members, which leads to social media, more money, more recognition.
- Thriving ministries that take time to learn about their people, help people not get lost in the crowd. They take the time to care and show that they care.
- I think the thriving churches are those ministries who are committed to doing the work of God such as, feeding the hungry, visiting the sick, ministering to those who are imprisoned. Those churches who are letting the love of God show through the ministries and members they serve are thriving. Ministries who are intentional on evangelism and being Christ to the community are those who are thriving. The dying churches are those who are

internally focused, who will not allow God to be God to them, who are not committed to the Word of God, who will not evangelize—who are everything they are not supposed to be. Churches who act like an organization rather than an organism are dying.

- Churches die that rely on the flesh and religiosity, traditions, and doctrines of men to operate. They do not rely on the Spirit to do His work in folks but man's.

- Some churches thrive because of great preaching, teaching, worship experience, and by word of mouth. On the flip side, many churches fail because of the lack of marketing by the members or the leadership. When people experience something that's good or great, they are compelled to share it.

- Depends on what's feeding them. I will relate this to my business, event planning business. This is something I truly believe in, we decorate that is my quality, someone else may cater the food, take pictures, DJ, etc. and if we do the best of OUR quality, we will have a great event, but if I try to do EVERYTHING myself, we will not have a great event, as only one person is leading. Like a church, you cannot be a pastor and deacon, etc. You need to have other people in the church actively doing their best and their part with their talents and someone that God sent to you for those purposes and develop those gifts to someone. Sometimes we get so excited, we go ahead of ourselves, put the wrong person in position, and take our eyes off God. First Corinthians 12:12–27: One body but many parts.

- The churches that I see thriving (provided my definition of *thriving* matches the one in the question) have been congregations with the least number of members, two hundred members or less. The way I view thriving is growing in their spiritual walk, meaning their connection to God. For me, evidence of spiritual growth is praising and worshiping God freely, in the form and fashion that the individual expresses or chooses, so long as it aligns with the Bible. Allowing an individual to seek HIM out at their own pace, as opposed to forcing a timeline of growth. Churches where the pastor leads the congregation in this way have higher success rates of individual breakthrough, healing, and a stronger connection to God. That, to me, is a thriving church.

- The area and demographic can have a lot of money. Everyone is looking for spiritual guidance and how much can you afford. If the church looks like a shack, then it will attract that demographic; if it looks nice, different demographics will come and support. Also, spiritually, some pastors are good at luring you in but not keeping the parishioners. Sometimes the congregation testimonies sound deeper than the pastor's sermon.

- Some churches thrive because the basic principle of LOVE, as said before, and people are welcomed. Also, that their words are backed up by action. The church is rooted in the word. We need one another, and everyone is supposed to be okay. Some churches thrive via corruption. Entangling themselves in the world. They have the money and flash and glitz and glamour of fakeness. In essence, they are actually dying spiritually. Some churches die due to the lack of love, care, and compassion for people. If people do not receive the love, they will seek the love somewhere else. Just like any relationship. LOVE.

REFLECT

_____

_____

_____

_____

_____

_____

_____

_____

_____

_____

_____

_____

_____

_____

_____

_____

_____

_____

_____

_____

5. HOW CAN ONE OVERCOME MINISTRY BURN-OUT?
  * I think when you are happy with yourself and where you are at, you are not burnt out. I think it is more so people are fed up or had enough of the people in church and quick.
  * Prayer, fasting, so they won't be so dependent on one person's message.
  * Rotation is key. Music ministry can go on one Sunday and dance choir can go another Sunday.

- Self-care. I am learning to stay in my lane and only operate in those ministries that match my spiritual gifts. We burn out when we try to do things we are not called to do. When we operate in our spiritual gifts and calling, we can do it all day every day without complaint because the Spirit gives us strength to do so. But when we operate in areas that we are obliged to rather than what we are called to, we get burned out because those activities are contrary to our calling.
- Rely on the Spirit of GOD to do the work and the convicting. STOP browbeating folks and micromanaging the Holy Ghost. Leaders, you are NOT Holy Ghost Jr.! Give the Word. Love folks.
- A church leader should have the ability to rely on their brothers and sisters to step in if they need a mental break. When you must be there 24/7, that is burnout. The pastor is expected to be on the post. To miss a Sunday, you feel guilty. But you have to listen to your body that needs rest. If we are real, we ALL can usher and lead the congregation. Share a message. It does not have to be so structured and law behind it. There is so much law behind a lot of person's spiritual identity, and that's where burnout comes in. You created an image that cannot be recreated or redrawn. It's unrealistic.
- And let GOD do the rest!
- I believe that church burnout can be avoided by learning to say no.
- Take time out for themselves. You can get to the point you are so overwhelmed with life. For example, me being a mother, daughter, wife, businessowner, trying to find time for myself (i.e., workout). My best method is to step back and spend time with me; that moment you spend time with yourself, you get that fresh anointing, you get

refreshed, get a fresh evaluation of self. Being selfish is being selfless, you are being selfish for the moment so you can be selfless later. Being alone, being in that quiet place, God can pour into ideas and revelations. You have time to RECHARGE.

- Pray and listen to God's command! Or just say NO. Sometimes people take on more than they can handle just because someone asks them to. The right thing to do is to use integrity with God and ask what it is you should be doing. God wants us to be happy and live in abundance, not drained and depleted. HE wants us to be excellent in what we do. Prayer and integrity with the Lord help to keep one from ministry fizzle.

- Ministering can be a lot sometimes. There should always be second persons, a right-hand person who can step in if you need to step back for a minute. If you are overwhelmed and overexerted, it is going to show, and it will affect people. Step back to refresh ourselves and make sure that some that we trust is able to step in. A lot of people don't do that because they are worried about losing their spot or someone not doing it right. People will start to notice if you start snapping at people, etc.

REFLECT

_____

_____

_____

_____

_____

_____

_____

_____

_____

_____

_____

_____

_____

_____

_____

_____

_____

_____

_____

_____

_____

_____

_____

Where Are the Men?

6. IN YOUR OPINION, WHY ARE THERE SO FEW MEN IN THE CHURCH?

* The black family is broken. Fathers are not fathers anymore, communities aren't communities anymore, mentorship is not happening. People from the church are not doing soiling of the oats and cultivating the next generation. This generation, mom goes to church and dad stays home to watch TV. The boys in the house will think church is a woman thing.
* Word out on the streets is GOOD GIRLS are in the church; also word out on the streets is that the church girls desperately want a man, so men run from the church. Women become like vultures in the church; they seek men like men are animals to be captured. It is the black church that is keeping women single.
* Million-dollar question; men need discipline.

- In my opinion, it is because they go with the wrong intention, and when that does not pan out, they tend to not go anymore. Also, it takes time for men to find their place in the church. It is harder for them to get in it and grasp the concept of Christianity.

- I think there are so few men in the church because the local church has not found a way to effectively support them while simultaneously supporting women. Too often, the local church plays to the emotional issues, which women can easily respond to, but does not enforce the physical, which is easier for men to relate.

- The church is too effeminate. TOO much into emotionalism and feelings. Men are logical creatures. God does not want us to lose our minds when we get saved. The Word says it is with the MIND that we serve the Lord. So HOW is it that folks get saved and then want to LOSE their minds? Men cannot thrive and operate in such environments.

- I feel there are few males in the church because church can be pretentious. Men do not like to share their weaknesses and emotions. Men have huge egos. Men are to be leaders; they guide and tell. PATRIARCHAL. This day and age, men are suffering. You cannot expect a man to uphold all these things, and he is falling apart. The church avoids dealing with men's issues. Men are supposed to be strong. Even in the Bible, the men were strong. There was always a coverup. A woman is expected to be weak in church and struggle and need the man for help and assistance. A man is not to have any of those as needs. The church avoids our emotional beings. People wonder why there are preachers that molested boys. This is because there was a weakness being overlooked and not addressed.

- I believe that there are few men in church because game recognizes game. I also believe that there are a few men in church because of pride. Most men do not want to be told what to do unless they are ready for change.

- I think the role of men in church has changed. I have two sons. In this society, at a young age, we do not push our young men to go. From a big perspective, less people are going to church. There are less women in church too, but because there has always been many women in church and when cut in half we still do not notice because women have always been high in number. I push my sons to go to church, and when we praise and worship, I have them stand because God has done too much for us to sit down. God has brought us a long way, and they will stand and honor God. It is all about teaching boys lessons. A lot of people, men and women, are not going to church because they have not made church a priority. We do what we want to do.

- Good question! Yes, the women-to-men ratio in church is far and few in between. From what I have heard from men over the years, it is that church is too indoctrinated for their liking. These particular men have also said there are too many restrictions, and they don't trust the pastors with the tithes. They believe church to be a way for pastors to conduct fraud by collecting tithes for their personal use. These particular men don't attend church regularly anymore, but they did seek out a church in the past. Because of those reasons, they have since turned away from going to church.

- Because they are probably working. For a lot of men, the work week consists of seven days a week. For some reason, church became a female thing. The only man seems to be the pastor. I think more men became more lost because they were not taught the right guidance. Women were taught to turn the other cheek while men were forced to face the world and get the money. For the men, there wasn't enough guidance for men. Once they turn four-teen, the church does nothing for the young man. Unless they were in a two-parent home. That type of child will stay in church. But a child raised in single-mother life-style, he will give up because God is not doing enough in his eyes. He has wants and needs, and it makes him feel as though God does not love him. We need more pastors to empower the young men and men.

- I am so tired of seeing this. Everywhere I go, it is like, where are the men at. It is a big problem; I think half the issues in church would not be there. I feel like women have a harder time letting things go than men. I think men run things differently. Sometimes women are more emotional, and we can take things someone said the wrong way. I think because of today's society, it's harder for men to be humble and get to that level of bowing down. Men are seen as strong, can't cry, must be tough in the eyes of society especially in urban areas. Also, women push men out. We don't need you, we can do this, we can preach, etc. This is in general in society as well, and as women, we can do this ourselves, independently, and then the men will go. The worldly views can creep into the church. Also, the lack of men there discourages the few men in church, and they are not able to relate their feelings, emotions, and experiences to a woman and need a man in the church to speak to, and there is no one there. They will also eventually leave. It can be intimi-dating. They can't relate and do not feel as though they do not belong.

REFLECT

_____

_____

_____

_____

_____

_____

_____

_____

_____

_____

_____

_____

_____

_____

_____

_____

_____

_____

_____

7. *HOW CAN ONE RENEW A PASSION FOR CHURCH AFTER BEING HURT?*
   - Renew their passion for CHRIST.
   - My motivation is not to help one to renew a passion for the church. Having been in the church for so long, I see that it is the same thread throughout the churches. It may take some time, but the same experiences are everywhere. Every woman or man needs to just go if they want to go and not for any other reason.

- Seeking God personally and asking Him for direction.
- Realize that church is not about the people, it is all about your relationship with God. You are not putting all your faith in a person; you are putting your faith in God. Being around genuine people who are about God to strengthen your walk. It is nice to fellowship, and it will make the process a little better, so long as you keep your relationship strong with God. If there are great friendships that come out of it, that is a bonus, but my main intention to go to church is to continue to build my relationship with God.
- I think that only comes with a renewed mind of what the church really is—it's not the pastor, the choir, the leaders—they or we are components of the church, but if we can remember that the church is the body of Christ, called to do great things in this world for God, we can find a renewed passion for the church.
- My current church found me; I didn't find them. Over coffee, they asked me questions like, "What do you do?" and "Why do you want to be involved on the campaign?" I left my name and number, and the pastor of the church always checked in on me outside of the campaign. She invited me to come to her church and restored my faith in the church.
- A person will have to want to do it within themselves first. If you are not ready to receive it, it will never happen. Keep doing the good deeds, and hopefully, it will be recognized and restore your passion. I was found while they were doing their work in their faith. I went from a huge black church to a small black church who have people of all different backgrounds.
- Reevaluate and say to self, "Why am I here?" Sometimes we get distracted by so many people doing wrong things. Reevaluate why you are at the church. Is it for the pastor, choir, etc. or is it for the anointing God has for you at

the church? You do not want to cause someone else to stray away or go wrong, so we must be careful and check ourselves, reaction and emotions. If your light is dim, you will not be effective. When your light is dim and they come to you for encouragement, you can cause their light to become dimmer.

- Passion for church may be obtained through prayer if that truly is the desire of their heart. If they earnestly desire it, ask God to restore what was lost, and they will be guided to where they need to be, and healing will prevail.

- Must be ready. It is not anything that can forced. Your body and Spirit will know when it is ready. If you always had the passion, it never went away. You just need to be healed. And you will come back. I personally have not been back to a church because they are spiritually lacking and cannot grasp my spiritual maturity. I have not found one I have committed myself to.

- If we love God, then we love our brothers and sisters. No matter what they do, we are instructed to still love them, even if they hurt us. Sometimes it crushes me that when I finish praying and speaking to someone about Christ, I don't have a place that I can recommend them. That puts me in a position that I need to do something about it. There are souls out there that need to hear the Word. The Holy Spirit will use us to create change. God can use us to heal, regardless of us being hurt.

REFLECT

_____

_____

_____

_____

_____

_____

_____

_____

_____

_____

_____

_____

_____

_____

_____

_____

_____

_____

_____

_____

_____

_____

8. DO YOU SEEK AN ALTERNATIVE PATH OF FAITH?

- I have not sought an alternative. I've simply gone PRIVATE, with regards to my spirituality, and that has been the best decision I've made. It has put me in a place of peace. I now realize and embrace the fact that GOD is within me 24/7 and GOD has given me peace about going PRIVATE. He has made it known to me that He is proud of the decision as our relationship is stronger because of it. I would not trade any part of my today with my yesterdays. I am living my best life now. My life is a 180, totally opposite of what once was.
- I have not sought out an alternative path, but I have been to a spiritualist church which I loved. The medium was accurate with his message and resonated with my spirit.

- Yes, I have sought several different paths of faith. I allowed my soul to seek other paths and schools of thought. God was always present. The alternative path served as growth for my soul's sake. It taught me to love ALL for who and what they are. Brought me closer and deeper to God in a way not experienced in church. I am very grateful to have experienced the other paths or schools of thought, as I call it.
- I believe in Christ, but I do not believe in the Bible version of Christ. Christ was a Buddhist. He reached the supreme. Christ died for our sins. People need to understand more about Him and who He was and what He stood for in order to gain a heart of Christ. Christ was very intelligent, and He was teaching people to be supreme within. That is how you are free and connected. That is the true reason they ordered the "gag" on Him. He would not stop teaching. Need to connect with the Christ within and save yourself.

REFLECT

_____
_____
_____
_____
_____
_____
_____
_____
_____
_____
_____

_____

_____

_____

_____

_____

_____

_____

_____

_____

_____

_____

_____

9. WAYS TO COPE WITH PAIN OR HURT:
    - Go to therapy
    - Exercise
    - Enjoy outdoors
    - A lot of prayer and seeking God and singing and getting into His Word
    - Watch church on TV
    - Find the gap and start a ministry

REFLECT

_____

_____

_____

_____

_____

_____

_____

_____

_____

_____

_____

_____

_____

_____

_____

_____

_____

_____

_____

_____

_____

REFLECT

IN WHAT WAYS DO YOU BELIEVE YOU CAN BE A BETTER FOLLOWER OF CHRIST?

_____

_____

_____

_____

_____

_____

_____

_____

_____

_____

_____

_____
_____
_____
_____
_____
_____
_____
_____
_____
_____
_____
_____
_____
_____
_____
_____

REFLECT

IN WHAT WAYS DO YOU THINK WE CAN DO BETTER AS THE BODY OF CHRIST?

_____
_____
_____
_____
_____
_____
_____
_____
_____
_____
_____
_____

_____

_____

_____

_____

_____

_____

_____

_____

_____

_____

_____

_____

RELATIONSHIPS

As you can see, these experiences all stem from bad relationships; whether, family, coworkers, friends, significant others, relationships are the foundation of who we are. It is almost like a fray in fabric. If not sewn back with love and care, it will continue to shred and dwindle like the faith of many within the church. It is up to us to be the change that we want to see. Help to build trust again and build stronger bonds. Apologize where we have been wrong and forgive when we have been wronged. Even if we never receive that acknowledgement or apology.

Additionally, the most important relationship you will have in this life is a relationship with God. Take the time to evaluate your relationship with God. If you do not have your own personal relationship with God, start one today with praying the below prayer.

To one of the interview questions, **WILL IT MATTER TO ANYONE IF YOU LEAVE THE CHURCH (I.E., WILL ANYONE CARE, REACH OUT TO YOU, OR CONTACT YOU)? IF NOT, WHY NOT?** This response spoke most to me about relationships: "People will know that they need to reach out because it's how we build a relationship. Another point where one needs to evaluate. People's problem is that they did not communicate or make relationships with anyone. What have you invested in? What events did you go besides Sunday and Wednesday services? Or did you just leave right after church? Are you an active member, or are you a pew warmer?"

REFLECT

What is your definition of relationship? What are your expectations? Do you communicate your needs or expectations? Why or why not?

_____

_____

_____

_____

_____

_____

_____

_____

_____

_____

_____

_____

_____

_____

_____

_____

_____

_____

_____

_____

_____

_____

_____

_____

_____

APPENDIX
EMOTIONAL WORD BANK

At times, we need language and words to put to our emotions and help us dig deeper. Below is an emotion and feeling wheel created by The Junto Institute.[4]

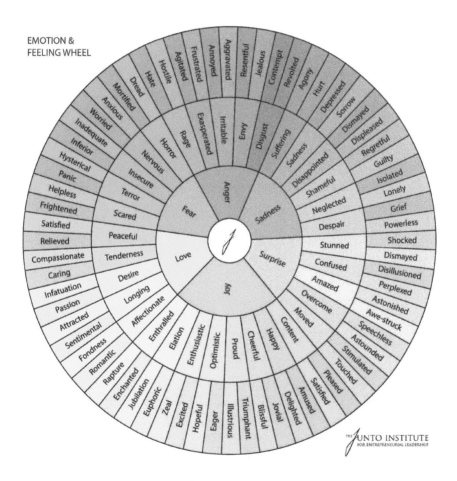

EMOTION & FEELING WHEEL

---

[4] Emotion and Feeling Wheel from https://www.thejuntoinstitute.com/blog/the-junto-emotion-wheel-why-and-how-we-use-it

RESOURCES

Below are helpful resources to assist you with self-care and mental wellness.

Find a Therapist
www.psychologytoday.com/us
www.psychologytoday.com/intl

National Suicide Prevention Lifeline
1-800-273-8255
Mindfulness App
https://www.calm.com/

ABOUT THE AUTHOR

Contessa Brown is a Newport, Rhode Island, native, currently residing in Providence, Rhode Island. She is a spoken word artist, local influencer, motivational speaker, and mental health advocate. Contessa Brown is the Founder/CEO/Director of Café S.O.U.L. which just reached eleven years in business! She began Café S.O.U.L. to serve as a positive platform for the community to creatively connect and collaborate. Born on September 4, she has always been determined to deliver happiness, healing, and wholeness to every person she meets. She is a grad of Roger Williams University, holding an MS in leadership and BS in psychology. She is currently working on her masters in holistic clinical counseling from Salve Regina University in order to start a private practice in expressive therapy. Contessa anticipates leading the current and future generations to a new level of healing and mental wellness.